The Official World Of

Andy Lane

UNIVERSE

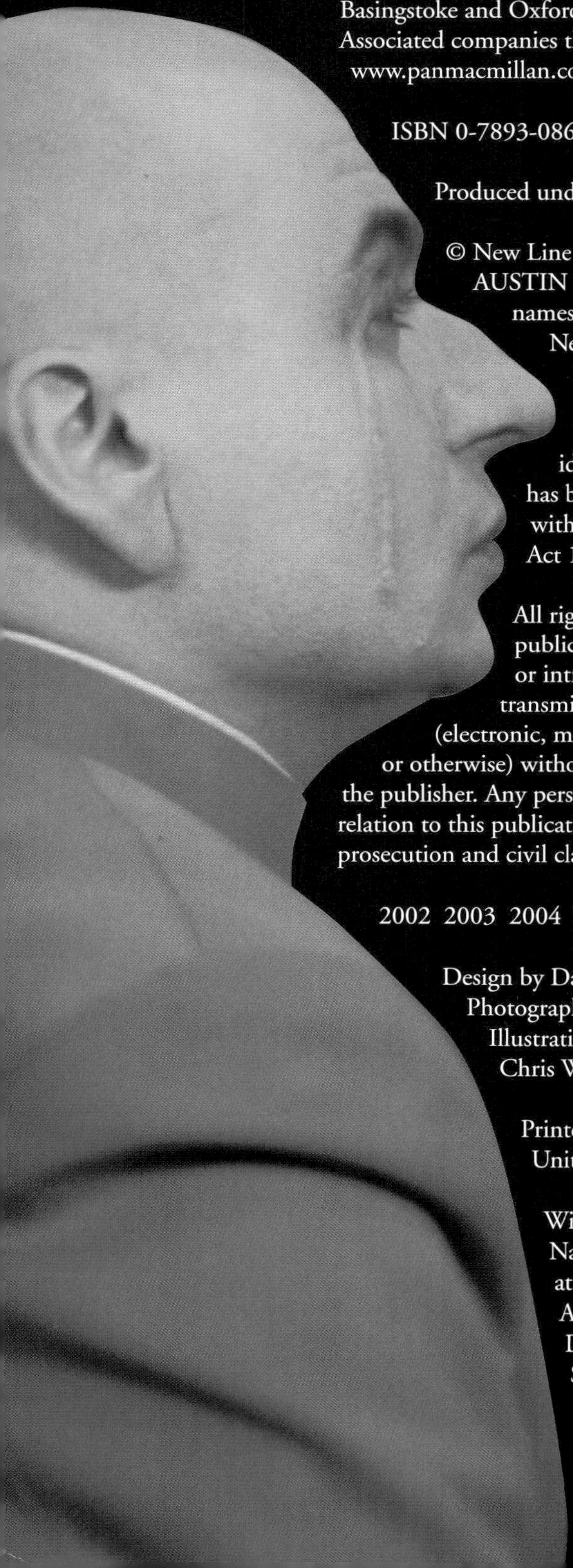

First published in the United States of America in 2002
by UNIVERSE PUBLISHING
A Division of Rizzoli International Publications, Inc.
300 Park Avenue South
New York, NY 10010

First published in 2002 in the United Kingdom by Boxtree
an imprint of Pan Macmillan Ltd
Pan Macmillan, 20 New Wharf Road,
London N1 9RR
Basingstoke and Oxford
Associated companies throughout the world
www.panmacmillan.com

ISBN 0-7893-0863-0

Produced under licence from New Line Cinema

2002 2003 2004 2005 / 9 8 7 6 5 4 3 2 1

Design by Dan Newman/Perfect Bound Ltd
Photographs courtesy of New Line Cinema
Illustration for 'The Swinger has Landed'
Chris West/Black Hat

Printed by Butler and Tanner in the
United Kingdom

With thanks to Dan Newman,
Natalie Jerome & Gordon Wise
at Boxtree; Marianne Dugan,
Amy Handkammer, Rachel Jones,
David Imhoff & Dave
Sztoser at New Line Cinema;
and, of course, Mike Myers.

The Official
World Of

AUSTIN
POWERS

Andy Lane

Contents

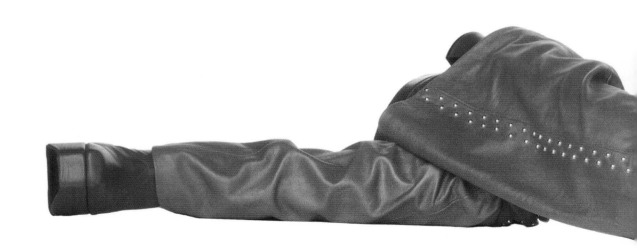

Groovy Baby!

FOXXY

5

Foreword

OH BEHAVE!

Time Traveller

'I CAN EXPLAIN… Okay, in 1967 Dr. Evil had himself cryogenically frozen. As a counter-measure, I too was frozen. Thirty years later we were both unfrozen. I thwarted Dr. Evil, got married, but found out my wife was a Fembot. I travelled back to 1967 because Dr. Evil stole my mojo. Evil got away. I travelled back to the future, caught Dr. Evil in the first act, only to have my father kidnapped and brought back to 1975…'

1960

1970

10 *Using an improv... time travel devic... Austin Powers (now* Sir *Austin Powers) travelled back in time from 2002 to 1975 in order to loca... his father Nigel, who ha... been kidnapped by arch-criminals Goldmember and Dr. Evil and hidden in the past. Austin was also captured, but escape... and returned to 2002 on the trail of the villains and his father.*

8 *Using an experimental M.O.D. time travel device, Austin Powers travelled back in time from 1999 to 1969 in an attempt to retrieve his stolen mojo… and failed!*

1940

1950

1 *Austin Powers was born in 1941. His father was the world-famous super-spy and International Man of Mystery, Nigel Powers. His early years were spent immersed in spy toys and gadgets – his father bought him a helicopter that fitted into a backpack – and so it was obvious that he would follow in his father's footsteps and become a world-famous super-spy and International Man of Mystery in his own right.*

2 *Following his graduation from British Intelligence Academy, Austin Powers established his cover as an international playboy and aspiring fashion photographer while mastering the tricks of the spy trade.*

3 *He also spent time in the Royal Navy in the early 1960s. Caught clap on weekend shore leave. Many of his missions were directly or indirectly associated with Dr. Evil, his one-time schoolmate and now arch-enemy.*

4 *In 1967, Austin Powers's naked body was frozen in a vault beneath the UK Ministry of Defence. Austin suggested this drastic move when he found out that his arch-nemesis Dr. Evil had been frozen in order to evade capture by British Intelligence.*

5 *In 1969, two years i... Austin's hibernation, of Dr. Evil's agents enter... M.O.D. vault, drilled in... capsule in which Austin's... lay and stole Austin's mo...*

Felicity Shagwell: 'Austin, what's the future like?'
Austin: 'Well, everyone has a flying car, entire meals come in pill form and the Earth is ruled by DAMN DIRTY APES!'
Felicity: 'Oh my god.'
Austin: 'Had you for a second, baby!'

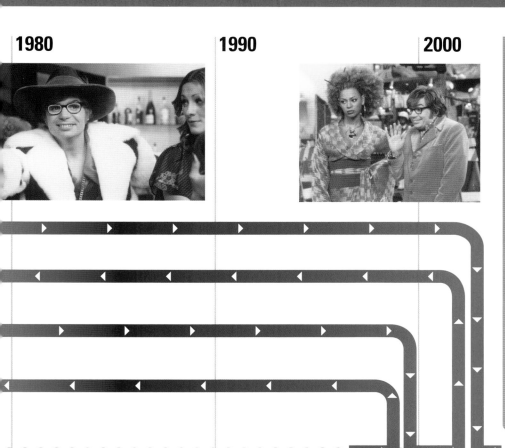

Austin: 'So, Basil, if I travel back to 1969 and I was frozen in 1967, I could go look at my frozen self. But if I'm still frozen in 1967, how could I have been unthawed in the 1990s and travelled back to the 1960s? Oh no – I've gone cross-eyed!'

11 *Austin makes a smashing return to 2002, mojo intact, sexy bird at his side, ready to embrace his existence in the present, with his new found family and all things groovy again. For now…*

6 *Austin's body lay inert for twenty-eight more years until, in 1997, British Intelligence information suggested that Dr. Evil had been reanimated. Austin was quickly defrosted to take on Dr. Evil once more.*

7 *Austin defeated Dr. Evil and settled happily into modern life. However in 1999 Dr. Evil sent Fat Bastard back to 1969 to steal Austin's mojo from his frozen body.*

9 *Austin returned to 1999 but – in a flagrant violation of all known laws of physics – a version of Austin that was ten minutes younger followed him back and seduced his colleague Felicity. When the impossibility of this was pointed out, the 'younger' version of Austin vanished. And the remaining Austin realized mojo comes from the inside and works its way out. Totally psychological, baby…*

'The 70s and 80s? Trust me, you're not missing a thing. I looked into it. There's a gas shortage and A Flock of Seagulls, that's about it.'

AUSTIN POWERS

Austin Powers — International Man o

THE YEAR IS 1967, and while free love reigns, Dr. Evil is up to no good. His most diabolical scheme has failed – and he wants answers. What's an evil doctor to do? He purges his organisation of unsuccessful henchmen with a push of a button and, as the conference table empties, Dr. Evil reveals his next plot – to destroy Austin Powers, jet-setting photographer by day and international man of mystery by night.

Along with his boss in British Intelligence, Basil Exposition, Austin hatches a plan to confront the elusive Dr. Evil. Austin deliberately walks into the trap set by Dr. Evil in London's Electric Psychedelic Pussycat Swingers Club and turns the tables. Never fooled by appearances, Austin, along with the swift judo moves of Mrs. Kensington, escapes an assassination attempt on his life by one of Dr. Evil's minions – all the while working the room and grooving to the 'switched on' music. Dr. Evil quickly retreats, escaping into a cryogenic freezing capsule within a rocket disguised as a gigantic Big Boy®. The Big Boy®, better known as the mascot of a popular fast food chain, launches off the top of the club, sending the frozen

After thir
years in
cryogenic
suspensio
Austin's a
had shru
considera

'Why must I b surrounded b frickin' idiots?

DR. EV

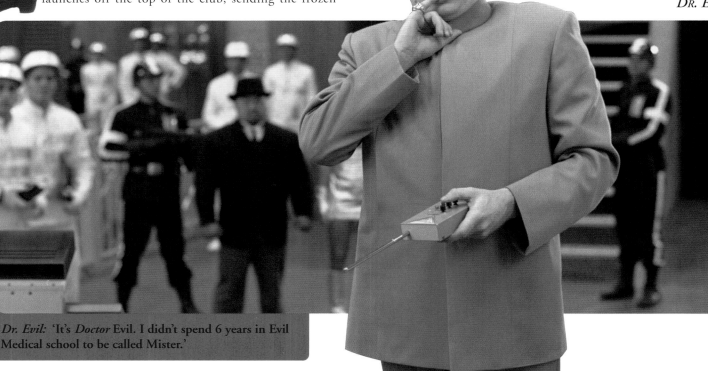

Dr. Evil: 'It's *Doctor* Evil. I didn't spend 6 years in Evil Medical school to be called Mister.'

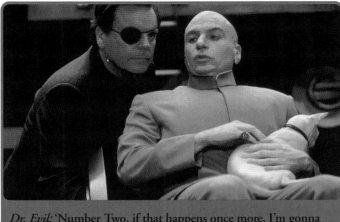

Dr. Evil: 'Number Two, if that happens once more, I'm gonna have your balls for breakfast, OK yeah… Denny's style, OK?'

'As long as people are still having promiscuous sex with many anonymous partners without protection while at the same time experimenting with mind-expanding drugs in a consequence-free environment, I'll be as sound as a pound!'

AUSTIN POWERS

Dr. Evil (and his beloved cat, Mr. Bigglesworth) into suspended animation. His aim? To return at a time when free love no longer reigned, and greed and corruption ruled again.

In 1997 engineers at the NORAD Combat Operations Center make a startling discovery – a Big Boy® rocket appears on their radar screens. Dr. Evil has returned, after a 30 year hiatus in space. Alerted by the US Air Force, Basil Exposition rushes to the British Ministry of Defence to thaw Austin Powers, who volunteered to be cryogenically frozen to await the return of Dr. Evil. This time around, Basil and company are fully prepared. With the help of Miss Vanessa Kensington, the daughter of Austin's long-since retired partner Mrs. Kensington, Austin is reanimated to resume his mission. Aside from going undercover with Austin, Vanessa is responsible for introducing him to the new decade in which he lives. 'You know, a lot's changed since 1967,' she warns.

Reclaiming control of his evil empire from his number two agent, Number Two, Dr. Evil is miffed to find that it has diversified into various legitimate money-making schemes under the banner of a company called Virtucon. Frustrated by the failure of all his plans to date, Dr. Evil issues orders that a nuclear weapon be stolen from

the former Soviet republic of Kreplachistan. He plans to burrow the stolen nuclear warhead deep inside the Earth using an underground torpedo in order to blow up the world. This plan, of course, could be terminated in the event that the United Nations were to pay him one hundred billion dollars. This figure, originally set at $1 million, was quickly recalculated to take into account the inflation rates for extortion since 1967.

Suspecting that Virtucon is a cover for Dr. Evil's schemes, Austin and Vanessa travel to Las Vegas, where they infiltrate Virtucon's premises but are captured by Dr. Evil's henchpeople.

In a final showdown, Austin Powers and Dr. Evil confront one another in front of Dr. Evil's underground torpedo. Dr. Evil orders the torpedo to be released, but Austin manages an improbably slow-motion dive toward the 'abort' button, hitting it just in time to destroy the missile just before it penetrates the hot, gooey centre of the planet.

While Dr. Evil escapes into space again, our hero and heroine relax in the glorious aftermath of saving the world, and the afterglow of their discovery of each other. And if Austin's world-saving dive was improbable, then his subsequent marriage to Vanessa was almost unbelievable. Austin Powers, the world's greatest swinger, committing himself to monogamy?

Austin Danger Powers

AUSTIN POWERS is charming and debonair. He's handsome, witty and sophisticated and is a world-renowned photographer. Women want him, men want to be him. He's a lover of love – every bit an International Man of Mystery.

While his toothy grin of twisted yellow choppers was captivating to women in the 1960s, Austin's appearance in the 1990s was in need of a little nineties make-over. Modern advances in dentistry were just another aspect of Austin's introduction to the future.

Alongside all his other skills, Austin is also a master of disguise. With only a few small props – a false beard, perhaps, or a turban – he can make himself completely unrecognisable, submerging himself in an alternate personality.

Suitable for randy babies to run their hands through

National Health gla...

Bad teeth

Frilly lace cravat covering sexy thatch of chest hair

One silver male symbol medallion (as if there was any question)

Italian boots, Bongiorno Boys!

'There's nothing more pathetic than an ageing hipster.'
DR. EVIL

Jiving down Carnaby Street, Austin brings music wherever he goes.

The personal effects that Austin put into storage when he was frozen give an insight into the kind of guy he is:
- One blue crushed velvet suit
- One frilly lace cravat
- One silver medallion with male symbol
- One pair of Italian boots
- One vinyl record – *Burt Bacharach Plays His Hits*
- One Swedish-made penis enlarger pump (plus credit card receipt, warranty and instruction book).

DO I MAKE YOU HORNY BABY?

'That's some getup you got there, are you in the show?'

BIG MOUTH TEXAN

'No, I'm English.'

AUSTIN POWERS

'I'm sorry.'

BIG MOUTH TEXAN

Who needs guns when you have cross mojo-nation?

It's Dr. Evil

DR. EVIL – Austin Powers's arch-enemy – has one aim and one aim only: to extort as much money as he can from whatever organisation will pay. To that end he normally threatens the world with destruction, but he isn't above a little blackmail to keep his organisation funded.

Dr. Evil has various characteristics which automatically mark him out as a psychopathic villain. He is fascinated by technology, for instance – huge drilling machines, sharks equipped with laser beams, seats that deposit people into fiery pits – and he loses patience with henchmen and subordinates very quickly.

Dr. Evil and Austin Powers have confronted each other on numerous occasions during the 1960s. Following a confrontation in London, Dr. Evil had himself launched into orbit and frozen in order to escape his nemesis.

Dr. Evil returned to Earth in 1997, to find that Virtucon – the legitimate face of his evil empire – was now a highly profitable organisation and that the semen he had left behind had been used to create a son – Scott Evil.

Dr. Evil and Scott had a rocky relationship from the start. Dr. Evil had difficulty relating to his son's slacker lifestyle, and considered having him killed on a number of occasions. Scott, for his part, had difficulty in understanding his father's over-elaborate ways of disposing of his enemies. They entered therapy for a while, but Dr. Evil had the entire group liquidated for insolence.

When Dr. Evil was frozen, he took his cat – Mr. Bigglesworth – with him. They had been companions for many years, and Dr. Evil wanted at least one familiar face around him when he was revived again. Unfortunately the cat lost all his hair as a side-effect of the cryogenic storage process.

> **'People have to tell me these things. I've been frozen for thirty years, okay – throw me a frickin' bone here. I'm the boss – need the info.'**
>
> *DR. EVIL*

Dr. Evil: 'No, no, no. I'm going to leave them alone and not actually witness them dying. I'm just gonna assume it all went to plan… Wh

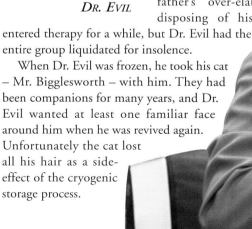

> **'At the age of fourtee a Zoroastrian name Vilma ritually shave my testicles. There really is nothing lik a shorn scrotum.'**
>
> *DR. EVIL*

Scott would often make rude gestures behind his father's back. In return, Dr. Evil often tried to have his son killed.

'My father was a relentlessly self-improving boulangerie owner from Belgium with low-grade narcolepsy and a penchant for buggery. My mother was a fifteen-year-old French prostitute named Chloe with webbed feet.'

DR. EVIL

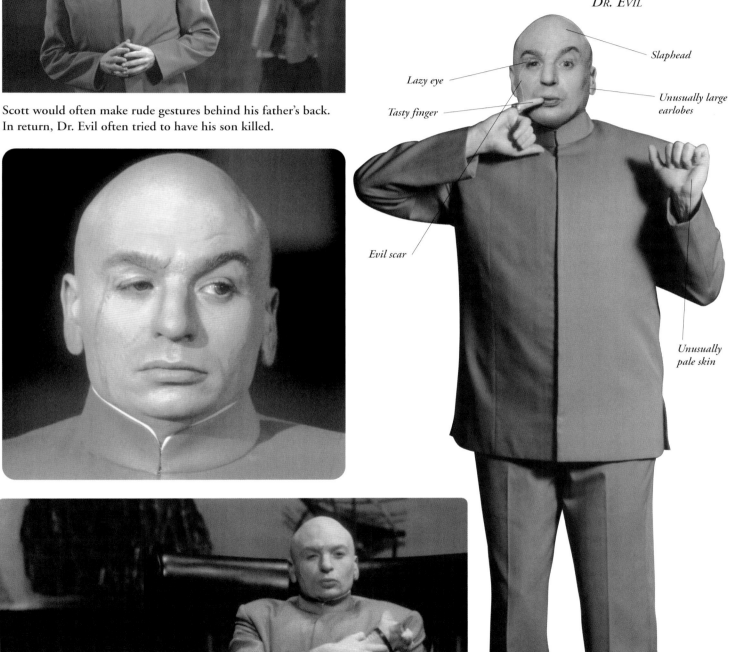

Slaphead

Lazy eye

Unusually large earlobes

Tasty finger

Evil scar

Unusually pale skin

15

Vanessa Kensington

Mrs. Kensington never posed for Austin – he did all the posing.

VANESSA Kensington's mother was Austin Powers's closest colleague in British Intelligence back in the 1960s. She never slept with him, but she obviously found him deeply attractive. Together they thwarted many of Dr. Evil's most diabolical schemes, but Mrs. Kensington retired following Austin's decision to pursue Dr. Evil through time by freezing himself.

It was some time before Vanessa could bring herse to ask how a penis enlarg pump actually worked.

Vanessa's oral skills were obvious to Austin Powers from their very first meeting – she was fluent in fourteen languages. She studied at Oxford, and joined the Ministry of Defence shortly after graduation, starting in the Cultural Studies section.

Vanessa is somewhat obsessive in her approach to life. When she packs her bags for foreign missions, for instance, everything is placed in its own little plastic bag and labelled. 'I'm the sensible one,' she told Austin Powers once. 'I'm always the designated driver.'

Vanessa found it difficult to relate to Austin Powers in the early days of their partnership. Previous bad relationships had resulted in some jealousy issues, and it took some time before she felt comfortable with Austin.

Thanks to Vanessa's sterling work aiding

Austin in foiling Dr. Evil's plan to activate every volcano in the world, Basil Exposition promoted her from the Cultural Studies section of British Intelligence to a position as an active Field Agent. She and Austin worked together on a number of other cases, and married three months later.

'My God, Vanessa's got a fabulous body. I bet she shags like a minx!'

AUSTIN POWERS

Vanessa: 'I will never have sex with you, ever. If you were the last man on Earth and I were the last woman on Earth, and the future of the human race depended on our having sex simply for procreation, I still would not have sex with you.'
Austin: 'What's your point, Vanessa?'

On their honeymoon Austin and Vanessa worked through the positions in his version of *The Kama Sutra*, including The Wheelbarrow, The Praying Donkey and The Chinese Shagswing.

Austin Powers was shocked on his honeymoon to find that Vanessa Kensington had been replaced by a robotic look-alike designed as an assassination tool by Dr. Evil. The real Vanessa had, presumably, been killed by Dr. Evil's organisation at some stage in the two years between Vanessa and Austin meeting and their marriage. Basil Exposition claims to have known about it all along, but said nothing to Austin.

Austin keeps a wall-sized portrait of Vanessa Kensington in his London pad. His continuing feelings for her were what eventually drove him and Felicity Shagwell apart.

Vanessa: 'Maybe next time you should try foreplay!'

Skintight leather jumpsuit

Fabulous body

Basil Exposition

BASIL EXPOSITION is the Chief of British Intelligence, having held that position since the 1960s. That makes him Austin Powers's boss, and as such he has an almost avuncular concern for Austin's safety.

Although on the surface Basil Exposition seems to be the straightest, most ordinary man imaginable, there are certain things that set him apart from other men. He appears almost timeless, for instance, looking almost the same in 1967 as in 1997. He may also have odd, precognitive abilities – he knew in 1969 that Austin Powers had travelled back in time, although nobody had told him, and he also knew that Vanessa Kensington had been replaced by a Fembot before Austin did.

Another of Basil's odd little quirks is his compulsion to explain in very simple terms exactly what is going on at any particular point in time. This habit endears him to Austin Powers, who often has a very shaky grip on what's going on and needs to be constantly updated.

Basil is often to be found around new technology. He uses a picture phone in 1967 to communicate with Austin Powers while Austin is driving his car, and an updated computer video link to the same car in 1999. He often hangs around the British Intelligence laboratories, waiting eagerly for the results of forensic and pathology tests to come in.

'God speed Austin Powers.'

BASIL EXPOSITI

Immaculate buttonhole conceals acid-firing device

Cufflinks contain enough plastic explosive to destroy a small building

Gold Hunter Watch doubles as tracking device and GPS receiver

Creases in trousers sharp enough to slice through flesh and bone

Basil Exposition: 'Hello Austin, this is Basil Exposition from British Intelligence. Now I want you to find out what part Virtucon play in something called Project Vulcan. I'll need you and Vanessa to get on that immediately.'

Basil's mother – Mrs. Exposition – was 92 in 1997 and lives in Tunbridge Wells, England. Austin considers her rather ugly. 'No offence, but if that's a woman, it looks like she's been beaten with an ugly stick,' he said the first time he met her. 'Think if everyone were honest, they'd confess that the lady looks rather mannish.'

In an ironic twist of fate, Basil Exposition was actually at British Intelligence Academy with Austin Powers, Dr. Evil and Number Two. All four of them graduated in the same year – 1958 – but time and fate took them all in radically different directions.

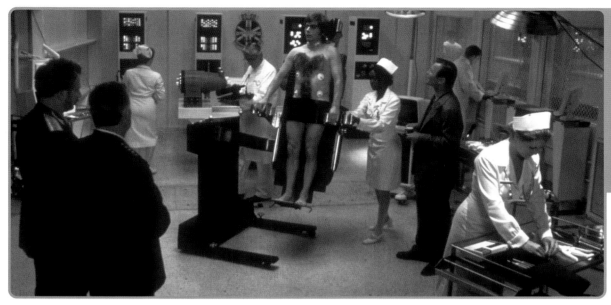

Russian General: 'So who is this Austin Powers?'
Basil Exposition: 'The ultimate gentleman spy. Irresistible to women, deadly to his enemies, a legend in his own time.'

Basil: 'Well, Austin, you stopped Dr. Evil from destroying the world with his subterranean nuclear probe, and somehow you and Miss Kensington have escaped unscathed from his evil lair and ended up on a raft.'
Austin: 'Well, that about sums it up, Exposition.'

THE EVOLUTION OF BASIL'S HAIR

Basil has aged remarkably well, apart from an initial spurt after graduating from the British Intelligence Academy. Often the only distinguishing feature is his hairstyle.

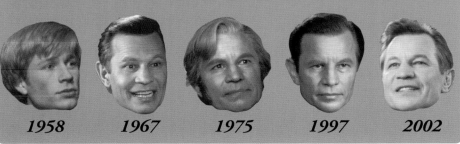

1958   *1967*   *1975*   *1997*   *2002*

Cryogenics Lab

DEEP BENEATH the Ministry of Defence in London lies a labyrinth of corridors and basement levels. In the deepest, darkest heart of that labyrinth, lies their greatest secret – the cryogenic storage facility.

The storage facility was originally created back in the 1950s as a means of storing away those people who would form the nucleus of a new civilisation following an atomic war. Separate vaults contain different categories of people – politicians, military officers, poets and celebrities.

Austin Powers was originally frozen in 1967, kept on ice not in the event of nuclear war but in case Dr. Evil ever returned to plague mankind. For two years Austin's frozen body was kept in a separate

Commander Gilmour: 'I hope your boy's up to it – we don't want to have to bail you guys out again like we did after dubya dubya two.'

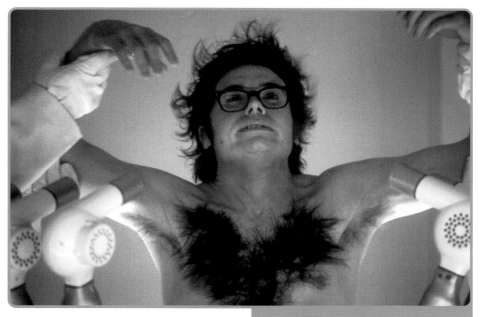

chamber, guarded by a regiment of the Scots Guards, but following a successful attempt to steal his mojo Austin's body was moved to the celebrity vault, where his body would be more visible and thus better protected.

Other celebrities stored alongside Austin included rap singer Vanilla Ice, stuntman Evel Knievel and former child actor Gary Coleman.

The M.O.D. cryogenic storage facility is manned twenty-four hours a day by scientists and technicians in protective clothing. The entire facility is powered by a nuclear reactor beneath the Cenotaph.

REANIMATION

The reanimation process includes several distinct phases:
- LASER CUTTING: the body is removed from its block of ice
- WARM LIQUID GOO: the body is defrosted
- REANIMATION: the body is brought back to life
- CLEANSING: the now living body is washed and blow-dried
- EVACUATION: the accumulated bodily wastes of many decades are voided. This can take some time.

'I've been frozen for thirty years, man — I want to see if my bits and pieces are still working!'

AUSTIN POWERS

SIDE EFFECTS

Revival from cryogenic freezing is a traumatic process. Potential side-effects include:
- cannot control volume of voice
- slight fever
- dry mouth
- flatulence
- loss of inner monologue

The Swinger has Landed

AUSTIN'S shagadelic transportation isn't limited to the ground. When it's time to hit the skies, Austin does it in style in his specially customised wide-bodied 747 jet. The 747's first-class cabin is a virtual psychedelic shag-pad in the sky, a 24-hour party for Austin and guests. Flying from coast to coast, country to country – whether it be in pursuit of Dr. Evil, or to induct new members into the Mile High Club, Austin's jumbo jet is the preferred method of transport as an International Man of Mystery.

It's easy to spot Austin's aircraft on the tarmac or in the air: it's the one with the day-glo paint job. Where most other international aircraft are liveried in drab white or regimented colour schemes, Austin's jumbo is a riot of orange, green and purple swirls. Austin's own symbol adorns the tail-fin, just in case anyone was in doubt that it's his aircraft. When Austin arrives in town, there's no doubt that the swinger has landed!

The cabin's lush interior décor matches the psychedelic exterior. Those splashy blues and yellows against the various animal hide upholstery is enough to bring out the jungle animal in any woman.

The dominant feature of the 747's main cabin is the circular, rotating bed. The bed has several safety features, including mink-lined handcuff restraints, which can be used in the event of turbulence, or to subdue over-randy passengers. As well as the circular bed, the cabin area also contained a fully stocked bar, capable of supplying anything guests might require.

Austin had his own swinging stewardesses in the 1960s, but when Austin was defrosted in 1997 he quickly discovered that things had changed. Not only were stewardesses now known as 'Flight Attendants', but they wouldn't wear his special uniforms and they wouldn't take part in the baby-oil fuelled orgies he had scheduled in place of an in-flight movie.

In Austin's private jet, it's always time for cocktails and shagging.

Psychedelic paintjob

'If you see this jet -rockin' don't come a-knockin', baby!'

AUSTIN POWERS

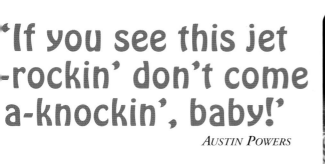

People who only saw the outside of Austin's jet thought it looked tasteless. People who had seen the inside as well thought the outside was quite restrained.

Groovy lighting

Rotating bed

Beanbags with seatbelts

Scott Evil

Scott Evil is Dr. Evil's son, conceived – or so Dr. Evil was initially told – in a test-tube as a replacement for Dr. Evil just in case anything happened to him. Given Dr. Evil's lifestyle, that seemed a likely eventuality.

What Dr. Evil expected was that his son would be just like him, but it didn't turn out that way. Scott Evil seemed to have no ambition apart from hanging out with his friends, listening to grunge music and watching porn movies.

Disappointed in his son, Dr. Evil made several attempts on his life. Some of them Scott avoided by accident, some were foiled by Frau Farbissina – one of Dr. Evil's closest advisors – who had taken an almost maternal liking to the boy.

Dr. Evil eventually relented, and joined a therapy group with Scott, but he quickly realised that the group was insolent and had them liquidated.

When Dr. Evil's scheme to explode a nuclear device at the centre of the Earth, unless he was paid a phenomenally large sum of money, was defeated by Austin Powers, Dr. Evil attempted to escape, using Vanessa Kensington as a hostage. Austin Powers was forced to put a gun to Scott Evil's head, but Dr. Evil didn't seem to care whether his son was killed or not.

Scott: 'I hate you! I wish I was never artificially created in a lab.'

Dr. Evil: 'Well, don 't look at me like I'm frickin' Frankenstein – give your father a hug!'
Scott: 'Get away from me you lazy-eyed psycho!'

'Remember when we froze your semen, you said if it didn't look like you were coming back we should try to make you a son so that a part of you would live forever...? Well, after a few years we sort of got impatient.'

Frau Farbissina

In therapy it's important to stick with it, waiting for a breakthrough, rather than killing the therapist on a whim.

'I haven't seen you my whole life and now you show up and want a relationship? I hate you!'
SCOTT EVIL

Uncharacteristic Evil hair

Ear stud

Slack lower lip

Unco-ordinated stance

Baggy trousers with plenty of pockets

Scott Evil: 'He comes back, and now he wants me to take over the family business.'
Dr. Evil: 'But Scott, who's going to take over the world when I die?'

Scott Evil: 'I was thinking, I like animals – maybe I'd be a vet.'
Dr. Evil: 'An <u>evil</u> vet?'
Scott Evil: 'No! Maybe, like, work in a petting zoo.'
Dr. Evil: 'An <u>evil</u> petting zoo?'

Number Two

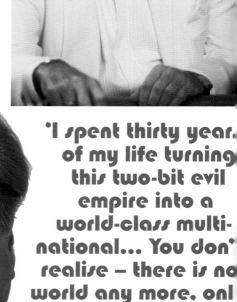

FOLLOWING the failure of a scheme to blackmail the world in 1967, Dr. Evil wiped out most of his 'evil cabinet' of advisors and went into suspended animation. Just before he froze himself, however, he brought in an old school chum to keep his organisation going whilst he was gone. That old school chum went under the pseudonym 'Number Two'.

For thirty years, Number Two kept Dr. Evil's organisation in one piece. Part of the time was spent in building secret bases and commissioning evil plans, but more and more of Number Two's efforts were devoted to legitimate business ventures.

For the first fifteen years that he was in charge, Virtucon (the name by which the world had come to know Dr. Evil's organisation) was a world-leader in the chemical industry. A sudden change of company policy in 1982 saw them taking over cable TV companies in thirty-eight American states, resulting in a massive increase in their share price. Virtucon also owned a steel mill in Cleveland, shipping in Texas, an oil refinery in Seattle and a company that made commemorative plates.

As relaxation, Number Two likes to gamble – usually with his confidential secretary Alotta Fagina. His winnings at the blackjack tables in Las Vegas were legendary, but owed more to technology than to good fortune. The eye-patch that made him look so rakishly attractive actually hid an X-ray scanner, allowing him to see through the cards and gamble accordingly.

Thirty years of holding the fort for Dr. Evil took their toll, however. Number Two had never really been happy with the idea of destroying the world, and found Virtucon's legitimate operations (supposedly just a front for money-laundering purposes and to put Austin Powers off the track) much more of a challenge. When Dr. Evil's scheme to flood the world with molten rock failed, Number Two cracked, accusing his former school friend of ruining his chances of making it big in the business world. Dr. Evil was forced to send Number Two plummeting into a fiery pit as punishment.

'I spent thirty years of my life turning this two-bit evil empire into a world-class multi-national... You don' realise – there is no world any more, onl corporations.'

NUMBER T

'Some plates, like the Cheeses of the World series, have gone up in price some two hundred and forty per cent, but, like any business investment, there is some risk involved.'

Number Two

Number Two: 'Mr. Powers, in this briefcase is one billion dollars.'
Austin Powers: 'You're eight hundred and thirty-two dollars short.'
Number Two: 'Well, I had to buy the case.'

Dr. Evil's Assassins

'My name is Mustafa and I am the man who will be killing you now!'

MUSTAFA

AN INTEGRAL PART of Dr. Evil's team is a mismatched set of assassins whose skills were all different but whose aim was the same – the death of Austin Powers.

Mustafa worked for Dr. Evil for over thirty years. Not only was he a trained assassin whose preferred weapon of choice was the knife, but he designed and built many of the technological gadgets with which Dr. Evil attempted to subjugate the world.

Mustafa designed the cryochamber that preserved Dr. Evil and Mr. Bigglesworth in space. However he was unable to anticipate feline complications due to the unfreezing process – the poor cat ended up completely hairless. Dr. Evil was swift to punish Mustafa: down the chute to the fiery pit he went. Despite terrible injuries, he survived and remained loyal to Dr. Evil.

Mustafa suffered from the odd psychological quirk that he could not bear to be asked any question more than twice, and would be compelled to answer after the third time. He sought psychological treatment for this problem, but the treatment was only partially successful, and he now has to answer questions after four times of asking.

Random Task – real name Sheung Kim – is a Korean whose expertise lies in throwing slip-on shoes with deadly effect.

Patty O'Brien's Irish heritage is the key to his character. A talented killer, he is also deeply superstitious and leaves items from his good luck bracelet – which also doubles as a garrotte – on each one of his victims.

'I can't recall your name, but the fez is familiar!'

AUSTIN POWERS

Dr. Evil's associates in 1967 included Rita, the hook-handed Don Luigi, Generalissimo and the lunatic surgeon Jurgen. He wiped them all out in a fit of pique.

'They're always after me lucky charms!'

PATTY O'BRIEN

Patty O'Brien died while trying to assassinate Austin Powers in a Las Vegas toilet stall. It's no way to be remembered.

Random Task occasionally thought about adding a high protein supplement to his diet.

'Ow! That really hurt. I'm going to have a lump there, you idiot. Who throws a shoe? Honestly! You fight like a woman.'

AUSTIN POWERS

The Conference Room

THE conference room is the nerve-centre of Dr. Evil's Las Vegas lair. Luxuriously appointed, almost sinfully comfortable, it has served as the base for his evil cabinet for over three decades.

The conference room, like the rest of the underground lair, has been carved out of the living rock. The rough-hewn granite has been left partially exposed in some areas as a concession towards modern design and also in an attempt to save money on wall coverings.

The centrepiece of the conference room is the immense table, around which Dr. Evil's advisors sit. The table itself contains a map of America, showing all of the legitimate holdings of Virtucon but also doubles as a dinner table with seven place settings. A communication screen set into the wall allows Dr. Evil to dictate terms to whichever government he wishes.

Dr. Evil: 'How do you like your quasi-futuristic clothes? I designed them myself.'

Abstract modern sculptures

Contributing to the calm, contemplative atmosphere of the conference room are the many works of art that are strategically placed around the walls – all of them stolen by Dr. Evil's organisation at various times. Most are modern art – smooth or spiky agglomerations of metal in abstract shapes. The only example of a more representational style – a bust of Wellington – was destroyed by Dr. Evil's henchman, Random Task, in a bravura display of shoe-throwing.

A set of buttons in front of Dr. Evil's chair allows Dr. Evil to tip any of his henchmen backwards and send them sliding down hidden chutes into a fiery pit located beneath the conference room. There they will – with a bit of luck – be burned to death. However, at least two henchmen have been sent sliding down the chute but survived the pit and later rejoined Dr. Evil's cabinet: Number Two and Mustafa.

There are several entrances and exits from the conference room. One leads to the living quarters (from which Scott Evil's music can be heard blasting); one leads to the main hall and one permits access to the Mutated Sea Bass Chamber. A fourth entrance – disguised as a rotating fireplace – connects to the Fembot room.

MUTATED SEA BASS POOL

Disposal of unwanted guests is a perennial problem for evil psychotics and would-be world despots. Henchmen can, of course, be discarded via one of the traditional routes – electrified chairs, chairs that tip backwards into fiery pits and so on – but opponents who work for the forces of good deserve something slower and more imaginative.

Dr. Evil's solution to the nemesis disposal problem was a pool full of mutated sea bass (scaled down from the original proposal – sharks with lasers attached to their heads).

Dr. Evil: 'What do we have?'
Number Two: 'Sea bass.'
Dr. Evil: 'Right…'
Number Two: 'They're mutated sea bass.'
Dr. Evil: 'Really? Are they ill-tempered?'

Dr. Evil was particularly fond of the Unnecessarily Slow-Moving Dipping Mechanism.

igh security
lephone link to
curity staff

Eliminator

Intercom

Trajectory to flame pit

Dr. Evil's Underground lair

FOR OVER thirty years the centre of Dr. Evil's operations has been located under several kilometres of solid granite just outside Las Vegas, Nevada. The base is only accessible via three heavily guarded entrances – a tunnel whose entrance is concealed behind a massive hinged rock; an emergency exit shaft and a deep silo through which Dr. Evil's escape rocket can be launched.

Austin's estimates of a three point turn to reverse the cart turned out to be wildly optimistic.

Dr. Evil's headquarters is manned by several thousand highly trained personnel whose loyalty towards Dr. Evil is unquestioned. It also holds the legitimate activities of Virtucon, a leading manufacturer of many items you'll find right in your own home. They make steel, volatile chemicals, petroleum-based products and decorative hand-painted theme plates for collectors. Virtucon runs informative guided tours of its underground facilities, which enable Austin and Vanessa to gain access.

'Ladies and Gentlemen – welcome to my underground lair.'

DR. EVIL

PROJECT VULCAN

Project Vulcan was the code-name for Dr. Evil's plan to blackmail the world for one hundred billion dollars (raised from one million dollars after Dr. Evil corrected for thirty years of inflation).

The key to Project Vulcan was the underground torpedo – a device with a massive drill bit which allowed it to penetrate the Earth's crust and deliver a nuclear warhead to the centre of the Earth.

The centrepiece of the base is the massive Project Vulcan Hall. This houses the electrical generators necessary to power the complex, the computer that controls it all, and Project Vulcan itself.

Dr. Evil's underground base was destroyed in 1997 when Dr. Evil himself triggered a nuclear self-destruct device in a last-ditch attempt to kill Austin Powers following the foiling of his Project Vulcan scheme.

Conveniently, the control systems for the Underground Lair include a clearly-labelled 'abort' button.

Dr. Evil: 'Gentlemen – I give you the Vulcan: the world's most powerful subterranean drill… so powerful it can penetrate the Earth's crust, delivering a 50 kiloton nuclear warhead deep into the liquid core of the planet. Upon detonation, every volcano on the planet will erupt!'

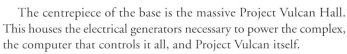

Fembots

OF THE MANY evil schemes perpetrated by Dr. Evil, perhaps the most evil of all was the creation of the Fembots. Macabre perversions of femininity, these robotic *femmes fatales* were specifically designed to appeal to Austin Powers. And did they? *Yeah*, baby!

Fembots are indistinguishable from glamorous 1960s housewives, with their blonde beehive hairdos, their frilly negligees, their furry, high-heeled slip-ons and their elbow-length gloves.

Dr. Evil's Fembots had one purpose – to destroy Austin Powers – and to that end they were fitted with various sets of armaments, from disorienting gas (emitted through nipple vents) to machine guns (firing through nipple barrels). If all else failed, they could explode (nipples and all).

Constructed from 1960s technology, the Fembots were finally undone by two things – superior 1990s technology and the timeless mojo of Austin Powers. Video recorder remote control units could send them into reverse and fast forward, as well as causing them to become mute and speak in foreign languages. They were also no match for Austin Powers's unbridled sexuality, which caused them to short circuit, vibrate like crazy and eventually blow up.

Austin believed that he had defeated all of Dr. Evil's Fembot army with his powerful mojo, but he was wrong. Somehow, Dr. Evil managed to replace Austin's new bride – Mrs. Kensington's daughter, Vanessa – with a Fembot copy.

'These are the latest word in android replicant technology. Lethal, efficient, brutal. And no man can resist their charms.'

FRAU FARBISSINA

Beehive hairdo covering central processing unit

Sultry blue eyes

Ballistic jubblies

Maribou mules

Austin thought he knew everything about female anatomy until he met the Femb

'Machine gun jubblies – how did I miss those?'

AUSTIN POWERS

Austin: 'Cold showers, baseball, Margaret Thatcher naked on a cold day…'

'I can't believe Vanessa, my bride, my one true love, the woman who taught me the beauty of monogamy, was a Fembot all along! Wait a tic… that means I'm single!'

AUSTIN POWERS

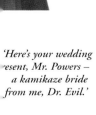

'Here's your wedding present, Mr. Powers – a kamikaze bride from me, Dr. Evil.'

When Austin Powers asked for Vanessa's hand in marriage, he was unaware of what the future would hold.

Austin the Happy Snapper

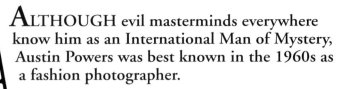

ALTHOUGH evil masterminds everywhere know him as an International Man of Mystery, Austin Powers was best known in the 1960s as a fashion photographer.

Austin was so successful as a photographer that women were desperate to model for him and then sleep with him – or vice versa.

Austin picked up his photographic career again in 1997, and once more shot to the top of the profession. Supermodels such as Rebecca Romijn and Ivana Humpalot begged for him to take their photographs, because they knew that a quick appearance in front of his lens would do more for their careers than an entire battalion of publicists.

Austin likes to invite two hundred close chums round for a spot of chick-painting.

'And I'm born ... and shoot! Born and shoot!'
AUSTIN POWERS

'You're an animal... You're a tiger... Now be a lemur, baby! You're a ring-tailed lemur!'
AUSTIN POWERS

Austin took some great shots of Ivana Humpalott, but lost his cool when she offered to return the compliment by shagging him rotten.

Smashing!
AND I'M SPENT.

Secondary flash

Firm yet sensitive grip

'Burrow, burrow! It's all you've got – you don't have sharp teeth capable of biting! Make an interconnected series of tunnels like the Viet Cong! And I'm spent!'

AUSTIN POWERS

'Crazy, baby! Give me some shoulder. Yes! Yes! Yes!'

AUSTIN POWERS

The Spy Who Shagged Me

1999, and Dr. Evil returns to earth after two years frozen in orbit. Once again he takes over the reins of his evil organisation, and discovers that since his disappearance his minions have again branched out into legitimate business and now own a successful chain of coffee bars. They have also cloned Dr. Evil, but the cloning process went wrong and produced a copy of him that was only one eighth his size. 'Breathtaking,' exclaims Dr. Evil. 'I shall call him Mini-Me.'

Dr. Evil's primary aim is, of course, to prevent Austin Powers from de-railing his plans to take over the world. First he attempts to kill Austin by replacing Austin's new bride – Vanessa Powers, née Kensington – with an exploding robotic replacement. When that fails Dr. Evil decides to steal Austin Powers's 'mojo' – his life force, his charisma, the power that enables him to defeat Dr. Evil time after time. Dr. Evil also decides that the best time to steal the mojo is thirty years ago, while Austin is still frozen and Dr. Evil is in orbit around the Earth. To that end he has developed a time machine, and he uses it to travel back to 1969 where he has an agent already working in the cryogenic storage establishment where Powers's body is stored.

Austin realises that his mojo has been taken when, in 1999, he is suddenly at a loss whilst attempting to seduce one of Dr. Evil's most seductive agents. 'Ivana Humpalot,' she introduces herself.

'I wanna toilet made of solid gold, Austin replies, 'but it's just not in the cards, now is it?' He alerts Basil Exposition, who sends Austin back in time to 1969 to thwart Dr. Evil's plans. Fortunately, 69 is Austin's favourite number.

Austin arrives at his own pad in 1969 and makes contact with Felicity Shagwell, an agent of the CIA. He also survives an attempt by one of Dr. Evil's agents – Robin Swallows (formerly known as Robin Spitz). 'Well, which is it baby,' Austin jokes – 'Spitz or Swallows?'

Felicity has discovered that a rogue agent named Fat Bastard has infiltrated the MoD. She sleeps with him and plants a tracker on his person, but he manages to get rid of it in a toilet

He's evil, he wants to take over the world, and he fits into most overhead storage bins. He's Mini-Me.

Austin: 'How do you get into the pants, baby?'
Felicity: 'Well, you can start by buying me a drink.'

at Paddington station. However, traces of a rare Caribbean vegetable in his stool sample, which he also left behind, lead Austin and Felicity to Dr. Evil's island lair.

Dr. Evil has taken full control of his 1969 organisation, and has developed a plan to put a giant laser, developed by the noted Cambridge astrophysicist Dr. Alan Parsons, on the moon and threaten the entire world with destruction. 'Mr. President,' he threatens, 'allow me to demonstrate the awesome lethality of the Alan Parsons Project. Fire the laser!'

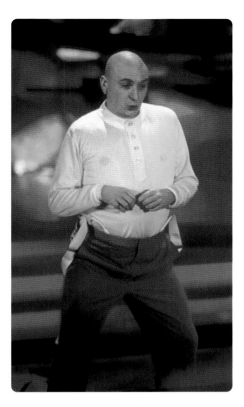

'I've got your mojo now, sonny Jim!'

FAT BASTARD

After sipping Austin's mojo, Dr. Evil hops on the good foot and does the bad thing with Frau Farbissina. Sadly, it all gets weird.

Austin and Felicity are captured by Dr. Evil's paramilitary forces and confront Dr. Evil and Fat Bastard. The two of them are imprisoned while Dr. Evil and Mini-Me travel to Dr. Evil's hidden moon base. 'You've all been chosen to be part of my Elite Moon Unit, which is divided into two divisions,' Dr. Evil tells his troops – 'Moon Unit Alpha and Moon Unit Zappa.'

Austin and Felicity give chase in a borrowed Apollo 11 rocket. Austin confronts Dr. Evil ('Alright slaphead – turn around slowly!') but Evil manages to take Felicity hostage. Faced with a choice over whether he prevents Dr. Evil's laser from firing or saves Felicity's life, Austin chooses to foil Dr. Evil's scheme. However, realising that he may have made the wrong choice, he uses Dr. Evil's time machine to travel back ten minutes and aid himself in saving Felicity's life and foil Dr. Evil's scheme. Unfortunately, Austin's mojo is destroyed in the process.

Dr. Evil escapes to 1999. Austin also returns to 1999, bringing Felicity Shagwell with him, having realised that his mojo had never been taken from him as true mojo comes from within.

Austin Powers: 'How could you sleep with Fat Bastard?'
Felicity Shagwell: 'I was just doing my duty, Austin. I had to.'
Austin Powers: 'No, I mean, literally, HOW could you sleep with him? He's so fat! The mechanics of it are mind-boggling!'

Austin Powers – Swinger, Baby!

DESPITE HIS years of sexual freedom, Austin Powers fell in love with Vanessa Kensington in 1997 during their mission to defeat Dr. Evil. They married and spent their honeymoon in France, but Austin discovered all too quickly that Vanessa had been replaced by one of Dr. Evil's Fembots. It exploded, almost taking him with it, but leaving him a single man again.

Austin's sexual prowess and sheer confidence were, he believed, the product of a strange glandular secretion that he referred to as his 'mojo'. When his mojo was stolen in 1969 by an overweight Scottish mercenary named Fat Bastard, Austin found himself suddenly unable to rise to the occasion. With his confidence and his libido gone, his only hope was to travel back to 1969 and find his mojo again.

Whilst in 1969 and unable to swing because of his stolen mojo, Austin built up a friendship with a woman for perhaps the first time in his life. Her name was Felicity Shagwell, and she was a CIA agent. Alas, modelling her behaviour on what she believed Austin would do in the same situation, she shagged one of Dr. Evil's agents in order to gain information. Austin was devastated, and didn't appreciate the irony that he had done exactly the same thing to Vanessa Kensington two years before, almost destroying their relationship.

Returning to 1999 with Felicity Shagwell, having defeated Dr. Evil, saved the world and realised that mojo was something he always had, Austin found himself in the middle of a strange ménage à trois. Another Austin Powers had travelled from 1969 to 1999, and the two of them very nearly ended up in bed together with Felicity.

'Austin Powers? He's the snake to my mongoose. Or the mongoose to my snake. Either way it's bad.'

DR. EVIL

AUSTIN'S TEETH
Modern dentistry has worked wonders on Austin's gnashers, but time travel seems to have a damaging effect.

1967   *1997*   *1969*   *1999*

Sorry ladies – he's lost his mojo!

Magnifying Specs – an invisible button on the hinge gives digital magnification

Martini (shaken, stirred, who cares?)

Symbol of male virility, also doubles as bottle opener

My Father Is Evil

FOLLOWING his abortive attempt to wreak volcanic havoc by detonating a nuclear device at the centre of the Earth, Dr. Evil once again returned to space and had himself frozen.

Arriving back on Earth two years later, he again took up the reins of his evil empire and set about blackmailing major governments – this time, by threatening to destroy Washington DC using a moon-based laser system.

In order to prevent Austin Powers confounding his plans, he stole Austin Power's mojo, thus rendering Britain's greatest agent useless.

Having missed thirty years of popular culture, Dr. Evil occasionally embarrassed himself by making accidental references to things he had missed. His naming of his moon-base the 'Death Star' and his laser system 'The Alan Parsons Project' drew derision from his son Scott, who had seen *Star Wars* repeatedly and held progressive rock in contempt.

Dr. Evil had believed that Scott had been created via artificial insemination using some of Dr. Evil's DNA, but he later found out that Scott was actually the result of a brief fling Dr. Evil had with his assistant, Frau Farbissina.

Whilst Dr. Evil had been frozen, his 'Evil Cabinet' had cloned him using the DNA he had left behind. The result was a copy of Dr. Evil, complete in every detail except that it was one-eighth the size. Dr. Evil called the clone 'Mini-Me', and grew more attached to it than to his son Scott.

Dr. Evil: 'It's how we drink it in Belgium. It's called a Belgian dip.'

'Don't mess with me – I'm one crazy mofo. I had to pop a cop cuz he wasn't giving me my props in Oaktown.'

DR. EVIL

'Look, we talked about this. We promised each other it wouldn't get weird. I can't let my feelings for you interfere with my taking over the world, you know that.'

'My dad's the head of a world-wide organisation that has aspirations for world domination.'

SCOTT EVIL

Dr. Evil: 'I'm the princess of Canada. Although I can't officially back that up with paperwork.'

'I've been a frickin' evil doctor for thirty frickin' years, OK? Cut me some frickin' slack.'

DR. EVIL

Further remote controls for the Evil Moon Unit

Remote control chair

Controls for chair: turn, tilt, raise, spin randomly around to cause nausea

He designs all his quasi-futuristic costumes himself, you know

Dr. Evil: 'Austin, I am your father!'
Austin Powers: 'Really?'
Dr. Evil: 'No. I can't back that up.'

Tight stockings to prevent space-thrombosis

Felicity Shagwell

FELICITY SHAGWELL is a CIA agent on loan to British Intelligence. She joined forces with Austin Powers when he returned to 1969 in search of his stolen mojo. Already waiting at his swinger's pad, she rescued him from Dr. Evil's assassins and drove him away to safety.

Felicity drives a Ford Mustang distinctively resprayed with a Stars-and-Stripes pattern, matching Austin's Union Jack Shaguar. She drives fast and hard, just the way Austin likes it.

Felicity believes in equality for men and women – and that means equality in all things, including the right to shag whoever you want, wherever you want. She is perfectly prepared to use her body to further her aims, even to the extent of shagging Dr. Evil's grossly fat agent Fat Bastard in order to get information on Dr. Evil's location.

Nervous at the idea of romantic entanglements or anything more than a one-night-stand, Felicity found herself attracted to Austin Powers as more than just a sexual partner. With Austin's mojo stolen, and with him unable or unwilling to do 'the mummy-daddy dance' (as he put it) she had fun with him, enjoying his ridiculous sense of humour and seeing the sights of London with him.

Although she found it difficult to admit, Felicity had secretly had a crush on Austin Powers since she was young. She studied his background, his methods and his accomplishments, and eventually joined the CIA so she could become a spy just like him. She even arranged to be transferred to London so that she could meet him, although by that time he had been frozen and she had to wait until he travelled back in time from 1999 to 1969.

'I shagged him. I shagged him rotten.'
FELICITY SHAGWELL

Co-ordinating female symbol medallion

Well-oiled zip

Ripcord – one yank and everything falls off

Kinky boots

'Felicity Shagwell by name, shag very well by reputation.'
FELICITY SHAGWELL

Felicity: 'Care for a ride?'
Austin: 'I'd love a ride, baby, but don't I need to get in the car first?'
Felicity: 'Oh behave!'

During their climactic attack on Dr. Evil's moonbase, Felicity was captured and imprisoned in a glass tube. Faced with the choice of saving Felicity or saving the world, Austin Powers saved the world, and Felicity died when Dr. Evil pumped poisonous gas into the tube. Realising that he loved her, Austin Powers used Dr. Evil's time travel device to go back ten minutes in time and rescued Felicity while his past self saved the world.

Felicity time-travelled from 1969 to 1999 in order to stay with Austin Powers. They spent a few happy years together, but Felicity eventually realised that Austin's heart still belonged to the late Vanessa Kensington. The two of them split up and went their separate ways, although Felicity stayed in what was actually her own future, as many of the feminist battles she had been fighting had already been won.

Felicity has a plan to get past the Single Inept Guard – she flashes her jubblies at him, and he falls in the magma.

Mini-Me

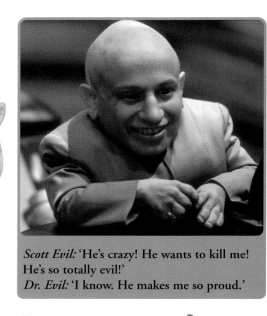

WORRIED ABOUT the possibility that Dr. Evil might die while in cryogenic suspension in space, his sidekicks hatched a plan to ensure that part of him would always live on. Using Dr. Evil's own DNA, along with an accelerated ageing process, they developed a clone of Dr. Evil, perfect in every detail. Every detail except size – for the clone was only one-eighth of Dr. Evil's size.

Mini-Me displayed many of Dr. Evil's own characteristics. He was similarly bald, he had a similar scar on his face and he adopted many of the same habits. He dressed in the same clothes – scaled down, of course – and he even adopted a very similar cat to the one Dr. Evil owned. He called it Mini Mr. Bigglesworth.

Scott Evil, Dr. Evil's son, and Mini-Me soon became locked in a battle for Dr. Evil's approval. Scott felt threatened by Mini-Me, and with good reason. The tiny clone tried to tip Scott's chair into a fiery pit, made faces at him behind Dr. Evil's back, drew nasty pictures of him and put a dead skunk in his bed.

Mini-Me was the first and last product of the cloning programme. Not only was he smaller than expected, he was also aggressive and sulky to boot. As well as his antipathy towards Scott Evil, he also displayed a vicious temper towards Dr. Evil's Number Two – Number Two – growling at him and biting him whenever possible.

During Austin Powers's assault on Dr. Evil's moonbase fortress in 1969, Austin mistook Mini-Me's silhouette for that of Dr. Evil, and attacked him. During the ensuing battle, Mini-Me wriggled inside Austin's spacesuit and writhed around like a ferret inside a pair of trousers. Eventually, Austin had to expel him into vacuum through a rip in the spacesuit's seams.

'Breathtaking. I shall call him... Mini-Me.'

DR. EVIL

Do you think he gives off a creepy Oompa-Loompa vibe?

'Oh, I can't stay mad at you. Look at that Punum!'

All evil genius lairs are required to have weird slow modes of transport. At least this one has a frickin' bell.

'He's tiny! I've had bigger chunks of corn in mah crap... it gives me the willies.'

FAT BASTARD

Dr. Evil's Time Machine

KEY TO Dr. Evil's plan to steal Austin Powers's mojo, or life force, was his time machine. Whilst the time machine developed by the British Government was portable, and built into a car which could then travel anywhere in time, Dr. Evil's was immobile and required two portals – one in each time period.

Dr. Evil first developed his time portal in the mid-1960s, before he was frozen for thirty years. His diligent team of evil henchmen, lead by Number Two, ensured that one portal was installed in the volcano lair they were building for him on a small Caribbean island, and another portal was transported to the moon and installed in the moonbase that was taking shape there – all part of his grand plan to blackmail the United States of America.

Dr. Evil sent his orders back in time through the time portal, from 1999 to around 1968. Based on those orders, Number Two ensured that everything was prepared for Dr. Evil's arrival.

> 'Ladies and gentlemen, I've developed a device for travelling through time, which I call a "Time Machine".'
>
> *DR. EVIL*

> 'If you have a Time Machine why not just go back and kill Austin Powers when he's on the crapper, or something?'
>
> *SCOTT EVIL*

Usually it's the evil villain's troops who wear the bizarre jumpsuits...

48

M.O.D. Time Travel Hangar

SEVERAL MILES outside London, England, in an unremarkable hangar far from the nearest town or village, the Ministry of Defence Special Projects Team is housed.

The hangar is so large that specially designed cars are needed to get round it. It is actually the biggest room in the world – dwarfing anything that NASA has to offer – but, as only thirty-eight people actually know of its existence (including the Prime Minister and the Queen), it will never actually make it into the Guinness Book of Records.

The MOD's time travel experiments began small, using Matchbox models of cars, but pretty soon they began to design cars

See, he's not really used to an automatic. Plus the whole point of being a secret agent is getting to break all the toys.

around the time travel equipment. The new Volkswagen design was a spin-off from this research, although all records of this fact have been suppressed.

The sheer size of the hangar is one of its most important assets. Although 99% of it is completely empty, the time-travelling cars designed by the MOD require a run-up of several hundred yards before their abilities come into play.

'This is smashing, Basil. I'll go back to the Sixties, recharge my mojo, defeat Dr. Evil and be back in time for tea.'

Austin Powers

Austin's Shag Pad

AUSTIN'S HOME before he was frozen in 1967, his 'shag pad' was a converted loft space above London's coolest, hippest shopping area – Carnaby Street.

The shag pad was home to a party that never stopped. In fact, the party continued on for another two years after Austin was frozen, and only wound down when he returned from the future and threw everyone out, saying that he needed some sleep.

Austin's shag pad occupied a two-storey space, with a balcony running all the way round the inside (accessible via stairs or, for the gymnastic, firemen's poles). All the structural beams and supporting members were painted orange, the walls were painted red and the floor was a psychedelic rainbow whirl. Day-glo beanbags were placed around the walls and a giant, circular bed took pride of place beneath an Andy Warhol print of Austin himself. A glitter ball completed the sophisticated yet raunchy feeling.

Faced with the prospect of a sure-fire Shagwell shag – but without his mojo – Austin loses control.

'It's my happening, baby, and it freaks me out!'

AUSTIN POWERS

Although Austin's shag pad was designed for pleasure, it was also a place of work as well. Somewhere behind the lurid paint and the glitter, Austin kept a darkroom where he could develop his photographs.

Following his defrosting in 1997, Austin moved back into his shag pad. The Sixties design quickly began to grate on him, however, and he had it redesigned in a minimalist white style.

When he travels back from 1997 to the Sixties, Austin reappears in his penthouse shag pad (in a Volkswagen) to find the party in full swing.

'What do you think of my shag pad, baby?'

AUSTIN POWERS

Above: the lift – for when Austin wants to go down. Right: even though his teeth look like muddy surfboards again, the slinky Robin Swallows makes a beeline for Austin as he reappears in 1969. Sadly she is working for Dr. Evil and makes several concerted efforts to top him. But of *course* Austin escapes – he's the International Man of Mystery.

Young Number Two

HAVING ESCAPED from the fiery pit into which he had been dispatched by Dr. Evil, Number Two wormed his way back into his leader's good graces. Perhaps Dr. Evil was swayed by the history the two men shared – after all, they had been at the British Intelligence Academy together, and Number Two had managed all of Dr. Evil's affairs during the thirty years in which he had been frozen and orbiting the Earth.

Despite his abrupt fall from grace, Number Two still hankered for an honest business career. He firmly believed that the organisation could make more money from legitimate means – including the sudden boom in coffee culture in the Western world – than in complicated nuclear blackmail schemes.

When Dr. Evil travelled back in time to 1969 he found a younger version of Number Two who had not yet been corrupted by the taint of honesty. Young Number Two was sharper and much more prepared to go along with Dr. Evil's plan to destroy Washington DC with a moon-based laser. Young Number Two's only drawback was the sudden antipathy that sprang up between him and Dr. Evil's clone – Mini-Me.

Following the collapse of Dr. Evil's scheme, Young Number Two

Number Two: 'Dr Evil, several years ago we invested in a small Seattle-based coffee company. Today, Starbucks offers premium quality coffee at affordable prices. De-lish!!'

'You're prettier than most girls I've shagged. After you pretty boy... I wanna look at your arse. Looks like two eggs in a hanky... You don't even have an arse. I never had such tendencies but if I did you'd be on my list.'

FAT BASTARD

'Dr. Evil, wouldn't it be easier to use your knowledge of the future to play the stock market? We could literally make trillions!'

NUMBER TWO

'Why make trillions when we could make... billions?'

DR. EVIL

used the time machine to travel to his future – 1999 – and there fell under the spell of his older self. The two had a short but intense relationship, one that abruptly came to an end when the laws of physics and morality caught up with them at the same time.

Number Two tried to make friends with Mini-Me, but suffered as a result; it turns out the little feller is a biter.

AUSTIN POWERS'S musical tastes run towards music for swingers and lounge lizards (Burt Bacharach, Elvis Costello, Quincy Jones), but he does front his own electric psychedelic band – Ming Tea. They got their first break in the mid-60s.

Ming Tea's five members have remained constant over the years, from their first chaotic recording session, through the long years of Austin Powers's frozen absence, to their highly acclaimed reunion tour once he was unfrozen again.

Some of the better known tracks by Ming Tea include 'Daddy Wasn't There', 'BBC' and 'Psychedelic Wah-Wah Pedal Funky Drummer Beat'.

One huge downer for Austin upon his revival in modern time was finding out that many of his grooviest rock & roll friends had met their demise; some due to drug addiction, some rumoured to have fallen victim to a rogue ham sandwich.

Ladies and gentleme
Mr Burt Bacharach!

'There's a sexual revolution, You can feel it in the air, People shaggin just like wease And they jus don't seem to care!'

LYRICS BY AUSTIN POW

Austin liked to let his wedding tackle swing free when he danced.

Austin's Desert Island Discs choice was surprisingly small.

Ladies and gentlemen I give you the one and only Ming Tea!

'BBC1!
BBC2!
BBC3!
BBC4!
BBC5!
BBC6!
BBC7!
BBC
Heaven!'

LYRICS TO 'BBC', BY MING TEA

Dr. Evil's Volcano Lair

GRANDIOSE ISLAND LAIRS are a standard accessory for the master criminal who wants to be noticed. Construction costs are immense, of course, and access is usually difficult, but there's a certain social cachet that comes of having one. And although there are many islands waiting to be transformed into lairs, not many of them come complete with volcanoes which can be hollowed out and converted into a fully-equipped base of operations.

The control room is suspended over a pool of liquid hot magma – so don't drop anything over the rail.

It is a measure of Dr. Evil's arrogance that he had the entire western side of the volcano carved into a likeness of his face, complete with scar and raised little finger. The main operations room is located just behind the eyes of the carved face, which act as windows from which beautiful sunset views can be seen. Dr. Evil's master chair is located just about where the pituitary gland would be.

In order to avoid the tedium of dealing with innocent holidaymakers or shipwrecked sailors who inadvertently land on the island, warning signs have been posted along the shoreline. The wildlife on the island is unusual for the Caribbean.

The master control room of Dr. Evil's volcano headquarters is lined with beaten metal and comes with a conference table, which also converts into a bed (complete with black drapes). The entire control room, and the ancillary living quarters around it, are suspended above a pool of molten lava (which, through ingenious design, also supplies all of the hot water and central heating in the base).

Due to the sulphurous emissions of the volcano, the entire base smells terrible. Air fresheners have been hung up to try and mask the smell, but, as Fat Bastard once pointed out, 'now it smells like someone took a shite in a pine tree.'

The volcano base contains two examples of Dr. Evil's technological genius – a time portal, through which he travelled back from 1999 to 1969, and a rocket with which he and Mini-Me managed to reach the moon before Neil Armstrong.

'Ah, Mr. Powers, Ms Shagwell – welcome to my hollowed-out volcano.'

DR. EVIL

Embarrassingly, Austin and Felicity had both turned up in the same style of bikini.

KEEP OUT
DR. EVIL'S PRIVATE VOLCANO ISLAND
=NO= SOLICITORS

Fat Bastard

FAT BASTARD is a freelance spy and agent of fortune who occasionally works for Dr. Evil. He's the incorrect weight for his height and he was born out of wedlock, hence the nickname. Fat Bastard's forthright manner and lack of social skills often mean that he causes offence, but he is, apparently, a skilled lover. He claims he has to be; given his size, it's the only way he can pull a bird.

Fat Bastard was sent back in time from 1999 to 1969 by Dr. Evil. His task was to act as an advance guard, infiltrating the British Ministry of Defence disguised as a Scottish soldier and determining where Austin Powers's frozen body was being stored. Once Dr. Evil had followed Fat Bastard back to 1969, the obese Celtic mercenary took the first opportunity to siphon off Austin Power's mojo and give it to his employer, then returned to 1999.

Fat Bastard may have links to the Scottish independence movement. He certainly has issues with the British and believes they have stolen Scotland's oil.

Felicity Shagwell managed to seduce Fat Bastard in London in 1969, and lured him back to her flat as part of a plan to place a bug on his person. She managed to introduce the bug successfully into an area that Fat Bastard would have trouble reaching, but she had to shag him first in order to get him undressed. And then afterwards as well, just so he didn't suspect anything. 'Ah'm dead sexy,' he told her later. 'You were crap.'

Fat Bastard will use any weapon that comes to hand, from a simple gun to a complicated set of bagpipes that emit knock-out gas. He can also use his vast bulk as a pretty effective weapon in its own right.

Fat Bastard often claims that his appetite is so vast that he once ate an entire baby. 'Ah'm bigger than you – ah'm higher up the food chain,' he says to Dr. Evil's miniature clone, mistaking him for a baby – 'get in ma belly!'

'First things first. Where your shitter – I got turtle head pokin' out!

Jacket spec tailore sewing sm ja tog

Austin's stolen mojo

Spe b poe

Cellulite (lots of it)

McBastard tartan

Argyll socks

'He's a disgruntled Scottish guard known for his lethal temper and his unusual eating habits. He weighs a metric tonne. His name is Fat Bastard.

DR. EVIL

Fat Bastard: 'Special Delivery!'

'Let me ask you a question –
are you happy?'

FELICITY SHAGWELL

'Of course I'm not happy. Look at
me – I'm a big fat slob. I've got
bigger titties than you do. I've got
more chins than a Chinese phone
book. I've nae seen ma willie in two
years – which is long enough to
declare it legally dead.'

FAT BASTARD

Baby – the *other* other white meat…

SORRY
I FARTED.

61

MiNi Me

MINI-ME
Height: 32in/81.2cm
Favorite (only) word: Eeeee!
Favorite food: Chocolate, especially
     Belgian chocolate
Defense mechanism: Sharp teeth
Genetic history: Clone of Dr. Evil

Scott, Evil Lite

Scott EVIL had only just managed to come to terms with the fact that his father was an evil psychotic who wanted to take over the world when Dr. Evil vanished once again from his life, having frozen himself in Earth's orbit. Dr. Evil was only gone for two years this time, but during that period Scott had become angry and rebellious, rather than just confused.

Scott Evil appears on an episode of The Jerry Springer Show called 'My Father Is Evil And Wants To Take Over The World'.

Scott followed his father back to 1969 in an attempt to patch things up, but he was distressed to find that Dr. Evil had already forged a semi-parental relationship with his diminutive clone – Mini-Me. Angry and confused, Scott retreated further into his shell.

'I wanted to tell you, but I had to hold it inside. You are my love child with Dr. Evil!'

Frau Farbissina

Scott found his father's efforts to name his various evil projects laughable. Having been frozen for thirty years, Dr. Evil did not realise that he couldn't call his laser-firing moon base 'a Death Star' without people remembering *Star Wars*, and that naming the laser itself 'the Alan Parsons Project', after the physicist who invented it, would invite comparisons with the progressive rock group of the same name. When Scott tried to point this out, he was quickly 'shush'ed.

Scott and Mini-Me shared an instant antipathy towards one another. Mini-Me made several attempts on Scott's life, and Dr. Evil did little to stop him. It was clear which one of them he preferred.

However, it was live, on national television, that Scott Evil learned the truth about his upbringing. Rather than being a test-tube baby, conceived in a laboratory, as he had thought, Scott was actually the naturally born result of a sexual liaison between Dr. Evil and Frau Farbissina. Having lost the respect and love of his father, at least he had his mother to look after him.

'I can't believe you'd do this to me on national television!'

Scott Evil

' I only came on the show as a platform to voice my aspirations for world domination.'

Dr. Evil

Scott: 'You're going to leave them alone with one inept guard. They'll escape. You do this every time!'
Dr. Evil: 'You forget that we're in a volcano, Scott. They're surrounded by liquid hot magma. I've been a evil frickin' doctor for thirty frickin' years, OK, so cut me some frickin' slack.'

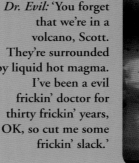

Dr. Evil: 'Scott, daddy's working okay? And when you're in the main chamber, try using your big boy voice.'

'You're not quite evil enough. You're quasi-evil, you're semi-evil. You're the margarine of evil, you're the Diet Coke of evil – just one calorie not evil enough.'

DR. EVIL

Because the laws of comic effect are more powerful than the laws of nature, skunks can be found way, way outside their natural habitat – on remote volcanic islands in the Caribbean, for instance.

Dr. Evil's Femmes Fatales

KNOWING THAT Austin Powers can be easily diverted by a pretty face, Dr. Evil has often recruited beautiful women to distract him, disarm him and even try to kill him. Austin Powers has, in turn, often attempted to seduce the women who work for Dr. Evil in order to get information out of them. It's very much a tit-for-tat arrangement.

Alotta Fagina worked as Number Two's confidential secretary for a number of years. Through him she got to know almost as much about Dr. Evil's plans as Dr. Evil did himself.

Alotta Fagina drugged and seduced Austin Powers on behalf of Dr. Evil, but had trouble bringing herself to sleep with Britain's top secret agent on account of the state of his teeth. She tried to stop Austin by threatening to kill Vanessa Kensington, but plucky Vanessa managed to judo-chop her way out of danger.

The Russian super-model Ivana Humpalot worked as one of Dr. Evil's agents, and also attempted to seduce Austin. This caused him a lot of distress when he suddenly discovered his mojo was missing.

Having travelled back to 1969 in search of his stolen mojo, Austin came across the dangerous Robin Swallows (neé Spitz). She attempted to stop him from meeting up with CIA agent Felicity Shagwell. When that plan failed, she orchestrated a murderous attack on Austin which involved knives, pistols, machine guns, cars and bazookas (not hers). Luckily Austin managed to save himself by repeatedly sheltering behind Robin. She ended up full of more holes than a broken sieve, and smudged her lipstick.

Basil Exposition: 'You're scheduled for a photoshoot, and one of the models works for Dr. Evil.'

Number Two: 'This is my Italian confidential secretary – Alotta Fagina.'

'Let's make love, you silly, hairy little man.'

ALOTTA FAGINA

Austin Powers: 'That ain't no woman – it's a man, man! It's one of Dr. Evil's assassins!'

66

Alotta Fagina: 'In Japan, men come first and women come second.'
Austin Powers: 'Or sometimes not at all.'

'You are hairy like animal! Make love to me, monkey man.'

IVANA HUMPALOTT

'Mr Powers, do you swing?'
ROBIN SWALLOWS
'Are you kidding? I put the "grrr" in swinger, baby!'
AUSTIN POWERS

The Alan Parsons Project

MANY OF Dr. Evil's plans to blackmail world leaders involved space or satellites of some kind. His scheme to build a base upon the moon and from there rain fiery death upon humanity was no exception.

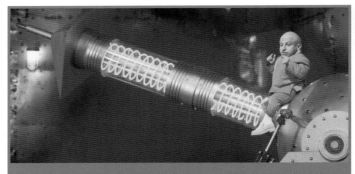

Dr. Evil: 'Okay Mini-Me, why don't you and the laser get a frickin' room?'

The building of a moonbase and the equipping of that moonbase with a massive laser system was all the more impressive when one considers that Dr. Evil's team accomplished the whole thing in 1969 – shortly before man's first recorded landing on the moon. In fact, it was advanced 1990s technology, sent back in time by Dr. Evil, that enabled Number Two and Frau Farbissina to reach the moon before Neil Armstrong.

The Alan Parsons Project was the key to Dr. Evil's scheme. A massive laser system, consisting of a gimballed barrel surrounded by a supercooled coil, it could be aimed at any spot on the Earth and fired. The actual firing was done by Frau Farbissina, dressed in a flying helmet and goggles and sitting in what appears to be an anti-aircraft gunner's seat.

Dr. Evil's moonbase was destroyed, and The Alan Parsons Project with it, when Dr. Evil triggered the self-destruct system in yet another attempt to kill Austin Powers.

'I'm sure Operation Bananarama will be huge.'
SCOTT EVIL

'You see, I've turned the moon into what I like to call a "Death Star".'
DR. EVIL

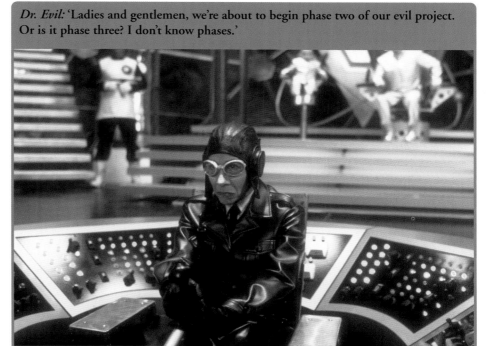

Dr. Evil's moonbase technicians working on the laser system while wearing fencing masks. What's that all about, then?

Evil Moon Unit

Dr. EVIL'S moonbase was constructed during the late-1960s, whilst Dr. Evil himself was in frozen sleep orbiting the Earth. Fleets of rockets travelled from the Earth to the moon, ferrying all the items necessary to sustain life in the cold, airless location that Dr. Evil had chosen as the staging post for his threats to destroy Washington DC. And all this before Neil Armstrong ever set foot on the moon.

The moonbase was constructed within one of the lunar peaks, which was hollowed out using high explosives and large shovels. The hollow peak was made airtight and pumped full of an oxygen/nitrogen mix. Apart from internal supporting members, little attempt was made to disguise the rocky walls.

The moonbase is oriented along an axis between two points – the landing pad for the rocket fleet, and the master control room containing the time portal and The Alan Parsons Project – the massive laser with which Dr. Evil would blackmail the President of the United States of America.

He may be small, but he's strong and vicious and he fights dirty. And Mini-Me isn't a saint either.

Dr. Evil: 'Okay – sick as a dog now. Gonna vom.'

Once the time portal was established within the hollowed-out moon peak, Dr. Evil used it to send the Alan Parsons Project back in time, from 1999 to 1969. Technology in 1969 was not up to the task of constructing such a device.

Also included in the design of Dr. Evil's moon base is an airtight tube which can be filled with poison gas at the touch of a button. The chances of Dr. Evil ever having the chance to use the tube in anger were thought to be slight at the time it was built, but Dr. Evil's foresight was proven when he managed to use the tube to kill Felicity Shagwell and thus distract Austin Powers for a few critical moments.

The waste disposal facilities are located half-way between the rocket pads and the main control room in the moon base. Storage and disposal of bodily wastes is a tricky problem in space, and Dr. Evil's design team solved the problem by allowing the waste products to be sucked out into the cold vacuum, where no-one would care.

'You've all been chosen to be part of my Elite Moon Unit, which is divided into two divisions: Moon Unit Alpha and Moon Unit Zappa.'

DR. EVIL

Austin Powers in Goldmember

DURING Dr. Evil's exile in space, Number Two went back to the drawing board to launder the evil empire called Virtucon into a 'legitimate' business – a Hollywood talent agency.

Since his plans for Preparation(s) A through G had failed, Dr. Evil decided to push on with his next plan, Preparation H. Dr. Evil explains to his loyal followers that he plans to travel back in time to 1975 and locate a Dutch scientist named Johann Van Der Smut. The roller boogie-ing Van Der Smut had an intense love for tight shorts, 70's pop culture and most of all, gold. His love of gold was so extreme that he lost his genitalia in an unfortunate smelting accident, hence coining his new moniker, Goldmember. Goldmember had designed a cold fusion tractor beam with which to attract meteorites towards the Earth but the technology in 1975 was not advanced enough for him to be able to build it. Once Goldmember was brought to 2002, Dr. Evil would be able use the tractor beam to attract the asteroid Midas 22 (constructed entirely of gold) to Earth.

Just when he thinks he is at the helm of a brand new evil plan, Dr. Evil is captured by Austin Powers before he can put his plan into operation, and is sentenced to 400 years in prison by the World Organisation.

For his latest acts of heroism, Austin Powers is knighted by the Queen. As he steps forward to receive this honor, he looks over his shoulder at all who have gathered to witness this tremendous event. Much to his dismay, he sees that his father's chair remains empty, still 'Reserved for Nigel Powers'. Unfortunately, his father's absence is not a new occurrence for Austin. Upon seeing Austin call to his father's empty chair, the room erupts in gales of laughter. A despondent Austin drowns his sorrows, performing a rocking set of tunes back at his shag pad. 'Daddy Wasn't There' is a huge hit with the crowd of Austin groupies.

During the party, Basil Exposition shows up and informs Austin that his father has been kidnapped from his private yacht, the *HMS Shag-at-Sea*. The only clue is that the Royal Navy sailors who were guarding Nigel Powers now have what Austin can only call 'Golden wedding tackle, gilded tallywackers... 14-carat trouser snakes...' – the calling card of the criminal mastermind known as Goldmember!

In their first face off since Dr. Evil's incarceration, Austin visits Dr Evil in Geneva, where he is being held under maximum security, to ask for information about Goldmember. In a quid pro quo tactic, Dr. Evil tells Austin, 'I'll give you Goldmember and you give me a transfer to a regular prison where I can be with my beloved Mini-Me.'

Dr. Evil reveals that Nigel Powers has been kidnapped by Goldmember and hidden in 1975 – twenty-seven years ago.

Austin travels back in time using Basil Exposition's time travelling equipment – a Pimpmobile – and

Dr. Evil's last scheme involved the moon. This one involves a moon – from Mini-Me.

'You have the right to remain sexy, sugar.'

FOXXY CLEOPATRA

infiltrates Goldmember's New York club, where he makes contact with former lover Foxxy Cleopatra. Foxxy informs Austin that his father is being held captive behind the scenes in the club, but Austin is also captured – it's all been a trap – and Goldmember uses Dr. Evil's time machine to take Nigel Powers back to 2002.

Austin returns to 2002, accompanied by Foxxy Cleopatra, but as he does so, Dr. Evil escapes from prison.

Austin discovers from Basil – who has a mole in Dr. Evil's organisation – that Dr. Evil and Goldmember are in cahoots and Dr. Evil's base is near Tokyo. Their plan is to attract the meteor Midas 22 to Earth and use the heat of its impact to melt the polar ice cap.

Austin and Foxxy rescue Nigel from Roboto Industries, which has built the Preparation H tractor beam, but Dr. Evil and Goldmember escape with the technology.

Discovering that he has been replaced in Dr. Evil's affections by Scott Evil, Mini-Me defects to the good guys and leads Austin and his dad to Dr. Evil's submarine in Tokyo harbour. Dr. Evil, meanwhile, demonstrates the awesome power of his tractor beam by dragging an American satellite to Earth and stating that he will melt the ice cap unless paid one hundred trillion yen.

Austin, Foxxy and Mini-Me infiltrate Dr. Evil's submarine lair and confront him. Dramatically, Nigel Powers reveals that he is Dr. Evil's father! He embraces his two sons and everyone is choked with emotion – except Goldmember, who is determined to complete the evil plan. Austin and his long-lost brother – 'Dougie' – combine forces, and together they reverse Preparation H's magnetic field, flinging the Midas 22 meteor back into space and electrocuting Goldmember by his own golden member.

Austin, Foxxy, Dougie Evil and Mini-Me head back to Hollywood to enjoy the premiere of *Austinpussy* – a star-studded film of Austin's exploits – while Scott Evil is left to take control of Dr. Evil's organisation…

Young Austin Rules!

AFTER HIS defeats of Dr. Evil and his numerous henchmen, Austin Powers is living the high life – being a true international man of mystery, cavorting with Hollywood royalty, out and about all over town, until danger surfaces once more. It's simple, really. Dr. Evil is becoming careless in his evil ways… being in space for so long, no one ever gives him a proper frickin' update. Needless to say, he leaves himself wide open for Austin's capture, and finds himself incarcerated. What Austin doesn't know is that he'll have to go inside the head of this lazy-eyed psycho to save his estranged father.

This 'time travel' around, Austin switches gears from the groovy 60s to the funkadelic 70s where he meets up with his old gal pal, the sultry Foxxy Cleopatra to rescue his father from the naughty clutches of the Dutch Roller Boogie King of Disco, Goldmember.

Austin seeks advice from his old nemesis, Dr. Evil. Old nemesis and one-time schoolmate, for they had both been at British Intelligence Academy together in 1957. Dr. Evil (then Master Evil) had been the front-runner for the International Man of Mystery award, but Austin had narrowly beaten him to it. The antipathy between the two men dates from that day.

Austin travels back to 1975, where his father was held hostage by super criminal Goldmember, then follows them back to present day Tokyo, where Goldmember and Dr. Evil are collaborating on a plot that might just destroy the world…

'Well, you might be a cunning linguist, but I'm a master debater.'

AUSTIN POWERS

Nigel Powers: 'You know, I think being frozen damages your brain.'

'I don't really like to use gadgets — outside the bedroom!'

AUSTIN POWERS

British Intelligence Academy

THE BRITISH Intelligence Academy is based in an ancient manor house in rural England. Its sole purpose is to educate the next generation of spies and secret agents.

The class of 1958 was one of the more interesting ones to have matriculated from the British Intelligence Academy. Austin Powers, Master Evil, Basil Exposition and Number Two all studied together, and their later careers were all intertwined in ways that they might not have believed possible at the time.

The supreme accolade that the Academy can bestow on its most successful pupils is the International Man of Mystery Award. Nigel Powers won it, and years later so did his son Austin – much to Master Evil's annoyance, as he had the best grades. Sadly Nigel wasn't there to see Austin receive the award.

Poor eyesight inherited from father

Thick luxuriant hair

Gob full of great big teeth

Simian chest hair

Fully functional mojo

Young Master Evil, just about to discover that he's been accepted into Evil Medical School.

'Boo-frickety-hoo. I had the best grades in the class, and I didn't get diddly-squat.'

Dr. Evil

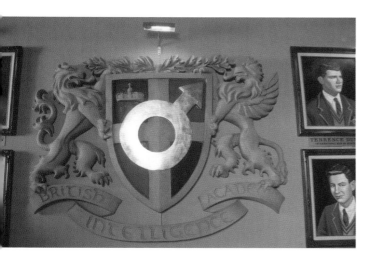

The crest of the British Intelligence Academy, flanked by portraits of previous International Men of Mystery.

French Mistress: 'Don't forget, Master Powers, later you have a brief oral exam…'
Young Austin Powers : 'Well, I hope it's mostly oral and not too brief!'

Dougie Evil

RETURNING YET AGAIN from deep space, Dr. Evil takes control of his evil organisation and sets in chain a plan to draw a golden meteorite towards the Earth. Before he can put his plan into effect his schemes are scotched by Austin Powers.

Dr. Evil is sentenced to 400 years imprisonment by the World Court. Initially he is placed in high security solitary confinement, but following the help he gives to Austin Powers in finding Austin's kidnapped father he is moved to a lower security prison and reunited with his diminutive clone, Mini-Me.

Dr. Evil and Austin Powers were originally at British Intelligence Academy together, along with Basil Exposition and Number Two. Master Evil shared a room with Austin Powers.

Whilst in prison, Dr. Evil manages to unite the various factions into one cohesive gang and, while they fake a riot, he escapes, using a key smuggled into him by Frau Farbissina – his former lover and the mother of his son Scott.

Dr. Evil was orphaned at an early age following the car explosion that killed his parents. Adopted by a Belgian man and his fifteen-year-old love slave, he was brought up by them to be evil.

Following his escape from prison, Dr. Evil takes up where he left off with his scheme to pull the Midas 22 meteorite to Earth. This time he has a refinement – the meteorite will crash into the North Pole, melting it and flooding the world unless he is paid a vast sum of money by the World Organisation.

Dr. Evil discovered that his son Scott, who had been running the evil organisation whilst he was in prison, had grown to be even more evil than him. More surprising is the revelation that Dr. Evil's father did *not* die in the explosion, and was in fact Nigel Powers. Austin is his brother, and Evil's first name is in fact Dougie. Turning against Scott, Dr. Evil sabotages his own evil plan and basks in the love of his 'new' family.

Dr. Evil: 'I can't believe I got caught in the first

'I was adopte by frickin Belgian for God's sake.'

DR. EVI

78

'D to the Rizzo, E to the Vizzo, I to the Lizzo'

DR. EVIL'S PRISON RAP

Fellow Prisoner: 'Man, I know guys on crack that make more sense than you!"

Austin Powers: 'Whoever kidnapped my father is a criminal mastermind, and there's only one person who truly understands the psychology of a madman – Dr. Evil!'

Austin Powers: 'Quick – how do we stop Goldmember?'
Dr. Evil: 'I'm not really a "hands-on" evil genius.'

Foxxy Cleopatra

FOXXY CLEOPATRA is a sassy FBI agent working out of New York in the 1970s. Working undercover as a singer/disco dancer in some of New York's hottest night spots, Foxxy penetrates her way through the scene to weed out the usual jive turkeys. Now she's back with a vengeance, working on her most important case to date: to put an end to the criminal mastermind with psychotic delusions of grandeur and flaking skin who 'offed' her partner – Goldmember.

Foxxy and Austin Powers had a relationship back in 1967, while Austin was on a mission in America. When Austin was frozen, in pursuit of Dr. Evil, Foxxy assumed that he had forgotten about her. But she never forgot about him. The fact that he showed up all those years later earned him a slap in the kisser.

Foxxy forgave him for disappearing without a word, and helped him escape an attack from Goldmember's gold-clad henchwomen. She then time-travelled to 2002 with Austin Powers to stop Goldmember and Dr. Evil from threatening the world.

How does she fit the Afro in that wetsuit?

'You've got a lot of nerve, dragging your jive white ass in here.'

FOXXY CLEOPATRA

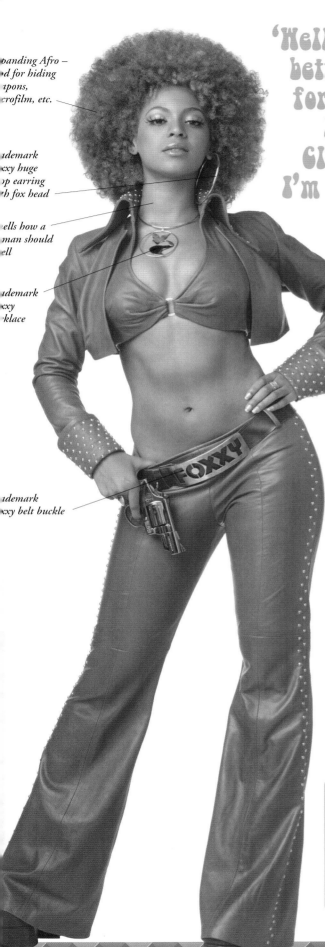

Expanding Afro –
used for hiding
weapons,
microfilm, etc.

Trademark
Foxxy huge
hoop earring
with fox head

Tells how a
woman should
smell

Trademark
Foxxy
necklace

Trademark
Foxxy belt buckle

'Well, the future better get ready for me, because I'm Foxxy Cleopatra and I'm a whole lotta woman!'

FOXXY CLEOPATRA

Foxxy Cleopatra: 'All I know is that momma got a taste of honey, but she wanted the whole beehive.'
Austin Powers: 'Oh beehive!'

When Austin told her that she was a dish, Foxxy took him a little too literally.

FOXXY'S HAIR

Foxxy Cleopatra always stays fashionable as she travels through time, thanks to her remarkably adaptable barnet.

Goldmember

A NATIVE OF Holland, the master criminal known as Goldmember was originally named Johann Van Der Smut. Trained as a metallurgist, he became obsessed with gold, to the point where his 'meat and two veg' (to quote Austin Powers) became gold plated during a freak smelting accident.

Goldmember: 'Oh that's a keeper.'

Goldmember's one over-riding obsession was the meteor Midas 22. Made entirely of gold, the meteor tantalised him, forever just beyond his reach. Determined to possess the largest chunk of gold in existence, Goldmember invented a 'tractor beam' in the mid-1970s that could pull the meteor to the Earth's surface.

Who remembers the 70s? The music... the roller-skates... the fashions... It was heaven just to be alive.

Goldmember's plan to obtain the Midas 22 meteor had one fundamental flaw – although his designs for the tractor beam and its power-source were workable, the technology did not exist to build them. Realising this, Dr. Evil travelled back in time and offered a partnership – he would provide advanced 2002 technology if Goldmember would assist in a scheme to blackmail the world.

Goldmember: 'Dr. Evil, before you take him away, can I paint his yoo-hoo gold? It's kind of my thing.'
Dr. Evil: 'How 'bout NO, you crazy Dutch bastard?'

Goldmember is an athletic disco-diva whose preferred clothes are spangly and snug in all the right places. He owns the Studio 69 club in New York (on the corner of 68th and 8th), where he regularly puts on demonstrations of his roller-disco skills.

With his freaky-deaky Dutch accent and an odd obsession with the idea of 'shmokes' and Dutch delicacies, Goldmember frequently flies into fits of sputtering 70s pop culture references.

Disgusted that Dr. Evil turns out to be not so evil, Goldmember hijacks the Preparation H tractor beam. Fortunately for the world, Austin Powers and Dr. Evil team up and manage to electrocute Goldmember by passing millions of volts through his golden 'tallywacker' (to quote Austin Powers).

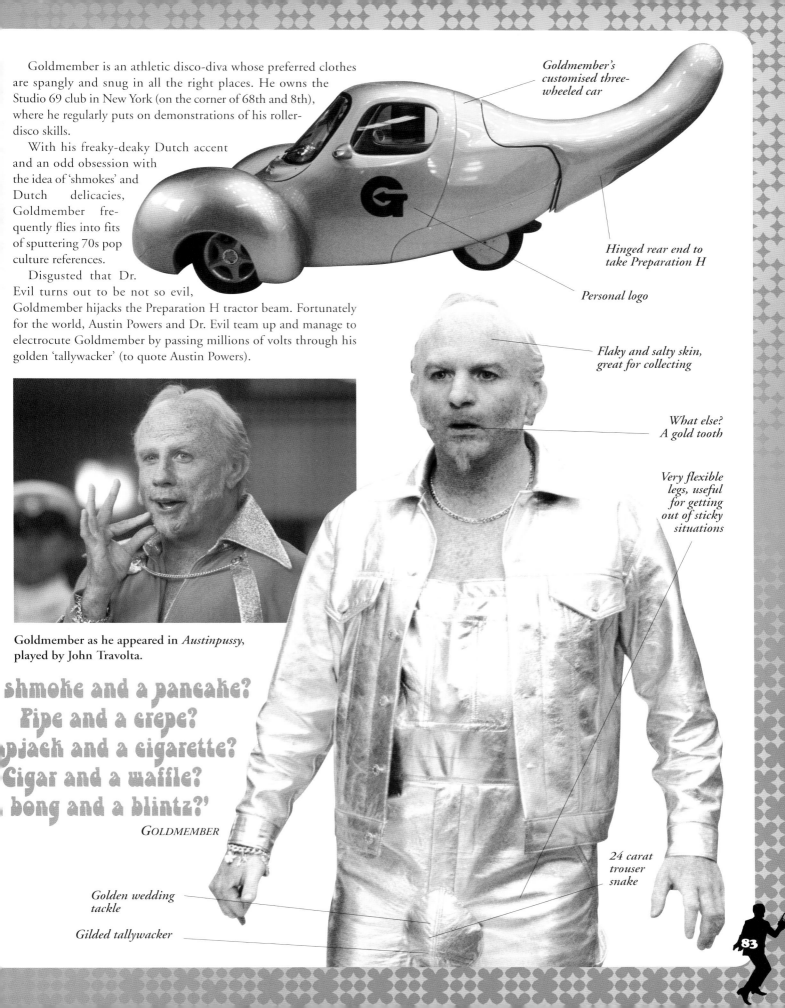

Goldmember's customised three-wheeled car

Hinged rear end to take Preparation H

Personal logo

Flaky and salty skin, great for collecting

What else? A gold tooth

Very flexible legs, useful for getting out of sticky situations

Goldmember as he appeared in *Austinpussy*, played by John Travolta.

'shmoke and a pancake? Pipe and a crepe? pjack and a cigarette? Cigar and a waffle? bong and a blintz?'

GOLDMEMBER

24 carat trouser snake

Golden wedding tackle

Gilded tallywacker

Studio 69

ON THE CORNER OF 68th and 8th in Manhattan stands a club that once was at the pinnacle of the disco movement. Studio 69 was where disco started and where it died, where the crazes and fashions and fads were invented, where the music blurred into the lifestyle and the lifestyle became the music.

The club's décor was gold. Everything was either made of gold, plated in gold or painted gold. Even the drinks had tiny gold flakes floating in them – don't ask where those came from…

Behind the scenes, the golden theme continued. Goldmember was obsessed with the stuff, to the point where he had become a master criminal, stealing all the gold he could get his hands on and allying himself with Dr. Evil to get more. Goldmember's office has a round bed in a revolving alcove, where Nigel Powers is held comfortably captive by Goldmember's henchwomen.

'I am from Holland – isn't that weird?'
GOLDMEMBER

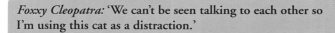

Foxxy Cleopatra: 'We can't be seen talking to each other so I'm using this cat as a distraction.'

'Welcome to Studio 69, Austin Powers. Excuse me while I change – the roller boogie has made me shweaty.'
GOLDMEMBER

Foxxy Cleopatra: 'He had the Midas touch, but he touched it too much. Hey Goldmember!'

'That's the way — uh huh, uh huh — I like it ... K.C. and the Sunshine Band.'

GOLDMEMBER

Frau Farbissina

FRAU FARBISSINA has been one of Dr. Evil's chief advisors for almost as long as he has been trying to take over the world. She was with him in 1967 when he froze himself to escape Austin Powers, and she was there in 1997 when he was unfrozen again. There is nowhere Frau Farbissina would rather be than by Dr. Evil's side. Or perhaps nobody else would have her.

It was Frau Farbissina's technical skill and twisted genius that led to the creation of the Fembots – metallic parodies of femininity designed with one purpose in mind – to kill Austin Powers.

Golfing is one of Frau Farbissina's few outside interests – outside stealing nuclear weapons and blackmailing the world. It was on the LPGA golf tour that she met the woman with whom she was to forge a close emotional relationship – the German golfer Una Brau.

What Frau Farbissina never revealed was that in 1969 she and a version of Dr. Evil from the future had shared a brief romantic interlude. Dr. Evil had drunk some of Austin Powers's mojo, and temporarily shared Austin's infallible ability to seduce women.

Frau Farbissina was in charge of collecting and guarding Dr. Evil's semen during his deep freeze in space. Years later, the emergence of Scott Evil brought about a great deal of speculation over whom his actual mother was. Was it test tube or Frau Farbissina?

Following Dr. Evil's capture by Austin Powers, Frau Farbissina visited Dr. Evil in jail and smuggled him in a key with which he could escape.

> **'Frau Farbissina – founder of the militant wing of the Salvation Army.'**
>
> DR. EVIL

Stern v

Tight li

Stern cl

Stern po

Strong vocal cords from screaming orders at henchmen

Surprisingly gentle hands

FRAU'S LOOK

Over the years Frau has stayed remarkably well-preserved. Being an evil henchwoman obviously does her good.

1967	1969	1997	2002

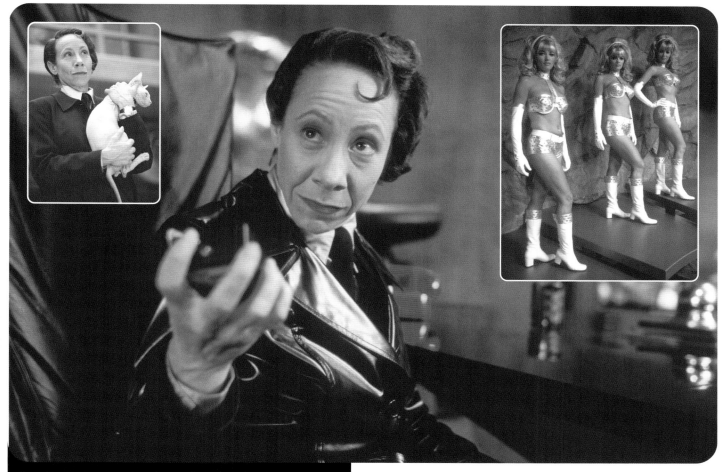

Frau Farbissina: 'Send in the Fembots!'

Frau Farbissina: 'I have come to embrace the love that dare not speak its name.'

'You know I'll never love another man again.'

FRAU FARBISSINA

'Yes, that's true...'

DR. EVIL

Dr. Evil: 'Nothing compares to this, being trapped in the belly of the beast night after night... Daddy's all pent up – Let's Freak!'

Daddy Wasn't There

FOR HIS EFFORTS in continually and consistently saving the world from Dr. Evil, Austin Powers was invited to Buckingham Palace by the Queen. She presented him with an array of medals then, to cap it all, he was also knighted, becoming Sir Austin Powers.

The investiture ceremony was held at Buckingham Palace, amid the pomp and finery of British Royalty.

Despite having promised his son that he would be there, Nigel Powers failed to attend. He had a history of failing to turn up for his son's proudest moments, having also missed the International Man of Mystery award ceremony in 1958.

Disappointed at his father's absence, Austin joined the party back at his shag pad, performed with his band and managed to meet Japanese fans. Before you can say, 'Threesome with Japanese Twins' Basil Exposition bursts in the room, informing him that his father was missing – presumed kidnapped.

The audience's laughter reminded Austin of his father's absence at his school award ceremony.

'Daddy! Daddy wasn't there, To take me to the fair, It seems he doesn't care, Daddy wasn't there!'

'DADDY WASN'T THERE' BY MING TEA

TV Announcer: 'Austin Powers, son of England's most famous spy – Nigel Powers – will be knighted by the Queen at Buckingham Palace.'

Nigel Powers

Nigel Powers: 'It's not the size, mate, it's how you use it!'

ONE OF British Intelligence's most capable agents, Nigel 'Adventure' Powers is legendary amongst villains and their henchmen world-wide. A well-travelled bon-vivant and man about town, his affable charm and cheeky wit disarm the opposition even before he starts to hit them.

Nigel Powers was voted International Man of Mystery by the British Intelligence College in 1944, eighteen years before his son Austin was honoured with the same award. He became one of Basil Exposition's best agents, and he was the inspiration behind Austin Power's becoming a spy.

While his son lived it up amongst the swinging psychedelic set, becoming famous as a fashion photographer and with his band, Ming Tea, Nigel Powers preferred to spend his time quietly enjoying himself with many female companions aboard his yacht, the *HMS Shag-At-Sea*.

Following a long and successful career as an International Man of Mystery, Nigel Powers was kidnapped in 2002 by Dr. Evil, transported back in time and hidden in a disco nightclub in New York belonging to Dutch archvillain Goldmember. While there, he managed to relax and enjoy himself with the bevy of beautiful henchwomen who were holding him captive.

There are only two things that Nigel Powers can't stand in the world – people who are intolerant of other people's cultures, and the Dutch. Nigel and Austin Powers share a secret language, known as English English, which allows them to talk without anyone who wasn't born within the sound of Bow Bells understanding what they are saying.

Despite their many physical and mental similarities, Nigel and Austin have always had problems getting on. All Austin has ever wanted is to gain his father's respect (that, and to shag Japanese twins), whereas Nigel can't abide whinging. Eventually they overcome their differences and admit their feelings.

'Don't you ever liquidate my son, understand?'
NIGEL POWERS

Nigel Powers: 'If you have an issue, here's a tissue!'

'Oh put those guns down. Is it your first day on the job or something? Here's how it goes: you attack me one at a time and I knock you out with just one punch.'
NIGEL POWERS

Not really stirred or shaken, so much as thrown together and slurped down before the glass gets wet

Trademark Powers teeth and glasses

Dapper dresser

Senior Swinger

Nigel is held captive in the Roboto laboratory and threatened with molten gold over the winky.

'Son, could you come back in, say, seven or eight minutes?'

NIGEL POWERS

Nigel gives his two sons, Austin and Dougie, a big hug.

Natty Threads, Austin!

AUSTIN POWERS is a true product of his decade, a 1960s man in thought, word, deed and paisley shirt. Having been unceremoniously thrust into the late 1990s, he has a lot of catching up to do. Fashions have changed and the market for flares has bell-bottomed out several times over the past thirty years. What sartorial delights has he missed? What fashion crimes have been committed in the interim? Can he remain a dedicated follower of fashion?

1975 Goldmember

1967 Austin

2002 Austin

1999 Austin

1975 Austin

1997 Dr. Evil

1975
Goldmember's
henchwomen

1997 Vanessa
Kensington

2002 Foxxy
Cleopatra

1969 Felicity
Shagwell

All drawings are
original production artwork.

Tokyo-a-gogo

ON THE SURFACE, Roboto Industries appears to be a successful Japanese firm specialising in high-tech machinery. Appearances can be deceptive, however, for Roboto Industries is actually one of the few firms completely dedicated to devising world blackmail plans for super-villains.

Roboto Industries provided Dr. Evil with costed designs, blueprints and circuit diagrams for Project Vulcan (a scheme to send a nuclear weapon to the Earth's core using an underground torpedo), the Alan Parsons Project (a scheme to destroy the world's cities using a laser based on the moon) and Preparation H (in which a meteorite was to be used to melt the polar ice cap).

Sadly for Roboto Industries, none of these schemes has ever actually been tried out for real, but were all foiled by Austin Powers before being put into action.

Failure to listen to the customer has been the undoing of many large companies, and Roboto Industries is no exception. Following his demand for more money from Dr. Evil for providing Preparation H, Mr. Roboto was unceremoniously dumped into a pool of sharks by Scott Evil.

Austin and Foxxy spot Mr. Roboto at the Asal Sumo Arena, where Fat Bastard is competing;

'Perhaps I should speak in English.'

MR. ROBOTO

'I have a feeling Mr. Roboto is lying to us.'

AUSTIN POWERS

'Tell me something I don't know.'

FOXXY CLEOPATRA

'I open-mouth kissed a horse, once.'

AUSTIN POWERS

Japanese technical excellence comes face to face with British engineering.

95

Dr. Evil's Submarine Lair

IN THE ULTIMATE act of hubris, Dr. Evil's submarine headquarters was designed as a massively scaled up version of Dr. Evil himself. The bald head provided a large degree of streamlining, of course. Even the periscope looks like the evil doctor.

As well as providing full conferencing and henchman destruction facilities, Dr. Evil's submarine was also the base for his Preparation H nuclear-powered tractor beam, which was located in the buttock area.

Ironically, the head of Roboto Industries – who built Preparation H – perished on board the submarine when he had the temerity to ask Dr. Evil for a bonus. Remarkably for an ocean-going vessel, the submarine lair has a pool of water in the main chamber, containing sharks with lasers on their heads.

'Welcome to my submarine lair. It's long and hard and full of seamen.'

DR. EVIL

Dr. Evil's plans for world domination finally went to his head...

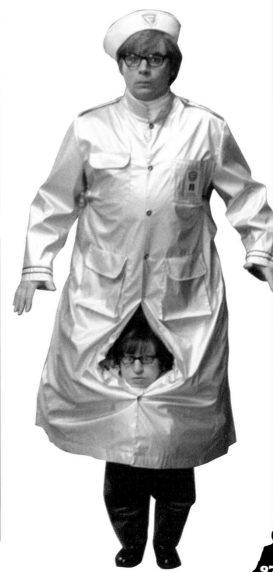

Can our fearless chums sneak in to foil Dr. Evil's plan before it's too late?

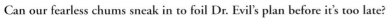

Fat Bastard Goes To Japan

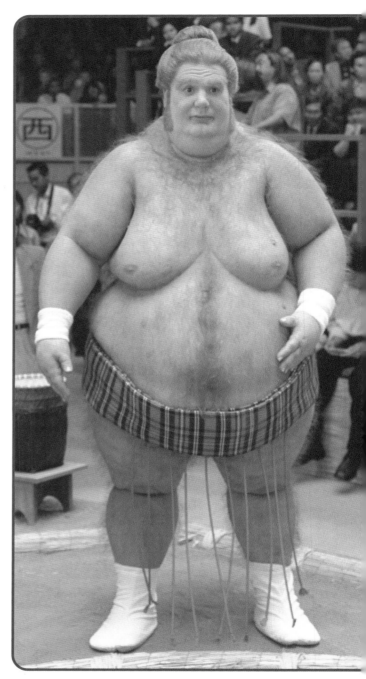

ALTHOUGH HIS missions to rid that meddling Austin Powers from Dr. Evil's plans had failed, Fat Bastard made a serious attempt to sort out his life. He realised that his massive girth, which he felt at one time was the core of his sexiness, was actually quite repulsive.

His solution? Go to Japan and channel the effects of his large size where it could be appreciated – the sumo ring. During this time, through many sweaty, stinking hours on the toilet, Fat Bastard thought long and hard about the trials and tribulations an 'oversized gentleman' like himself had had to endure.

Fat Bastard soon found that he enjoyed Sumo wrestling, and – better than that – he was actually very good at it. But despite his new happiness and success, Fat Bastard couldn't help slipping back to his old ways. He started working for Dr. Evil again, acting as a courier between Evil and his chief designer, Mr. Roboto. As before, he was never a part of Dr. Evil's organisation – he merely acted as a mercenary, providing services for money.

In his encounter with Austin, Fat Bastard attempts to appeal to Austin's sensitive side by telling him of his lifelong hardships as an obese person. However, these heartfelt sentiments are soon overshadowed by Fat Bastard's lack of control over his sphincter. That sphincter – it always seemed have a mind of its own!

Eventually he found a diet that worked – eating nothing but low-calorie sandwiches – and lost a lot of weight. Unfortunately he had a problem with all the loose skin, especially around the neck.

'This diaper's makin mah nuts rub together so much it' gonna start a fire!'

FAT BASTARL

Fat Bastard: 'Are we done here? I gotta take a crap.'

'Even stink would say that stinks.'

FAT BASTARD

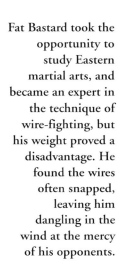

Fat Bastard took the opportunity to study Eastern martial arts, and became an expert in the technique of wire-fighting, but his weight proved a disadvantage. He found the wires often snapped, leaving him dangling in the wind at the mercy of his opponents.

The defection of Mini-Me

BY THE TIME Dr. Evil started working on Preparation H, he and his one-eighth size replica had become inseparable – it was all mini-trikes, chocolates and baby slings for the evil duo. Mini-Me could do no wrong, except when he dozed off in Virtucon meetings.

During his incarceration in high-security prison, Dr. Evil made a bargain with Austin Powers. In return for information on the location of Austin's kidnapped father, Austin would ensure that Dr. Evil was moved to a lower security prison where he could be with his beloved Mini-Me. Once reunited, the two quickly 'assumed their positions' as chief control freaks of the prison yard, and planned their escape with the help of the inmates.

Unbeknownst to the vertically-challenged Mini-Me, his 'big brother' Scott Evil decided to take over the family business during Dr. Evil's incarceration. Upon their return to the lair, Mini-Me was shocked and dejected by Dr. Evil's new found affections for his biological 'uncloned' son, Scott. Dr. Evil's neglect of Mini-Me gave prisoner Nigel Powers the perfect opportunity to swoop in and tell Mini-Me that, 'just because you're an eighth their size doesn't mean that you deserve an eighth of their respect'. That, paired with Nigel's blushing compliments on Mini-Me's 'unit' gave Mini-Me all the encouragement he needed to leave Dr. Evil's side and defect to British Intelligence. His first mission? To provide Austin Powers with the location of Dr. Evil's submarine lair.

Once Mini-Me joined Austin Powers in his crusade against Dr. Evil's schemes, he went right to work, even dressing as a pseudo-International Man of Mystery. Together, he and Austin infiltrated Dr. Evil's submarine but found only one disguise to wear. In a quick-thinking move, Austin perched himself on Mini-Me's shoulders and they carried on through the submarine. Things went without a hitch until they were stopped by the sub's henchman physician and dragged into an examining room for a physical, which required a urine sample. The jig was up and both Austin and his mini sidekick were on the run. Austin Powers was captured, but the elusive Mini-Me escaped into the submarine's ventilation system.

Dr. Evil and Mini-Me were reunited when Dr. Evil saw the futility of his continuing attempts to 'off' Austin Powers, and embraced his new found position among the Powers family.

'Horny bugger.'

AUSTIN POW.
PULLING MINI-
OFF FO
CLEOPATRA'S

Dr. Evil: 'Here's your chocolate. It was made in Bruges – that's in Belgium… Look at him, he loves it. It's like frickin' catnip for clones.'

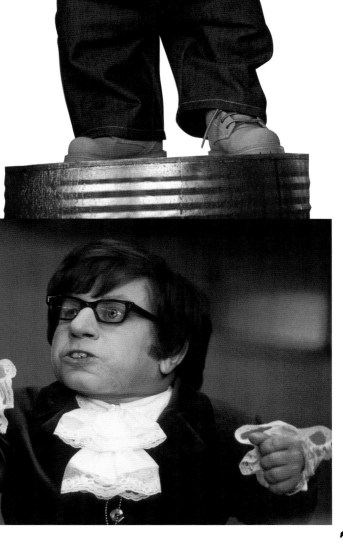

'Good lord, you're a tripod. What do you feed that thing? It's like a baby's arm holding an apple! Good news is, if you get tired you can use it as a kickstand!'

NIGEL POWERS, LOOKING AT MINI-ME'S 'GIGGLESTICK'

Austinpussy!

DESPITE HAVING won the International Man of Mystery award, and despite the fact that his career as a famous fashion photographer was meant to be a cover for his secret agent activities, Austin's work for British Intelligence was widely known. Members of the public would stop him in the street and thank him for saving the world.

Austin's adventures were immortalised on celluloid by Steven Spielberg in 2002, in the film *Austinpussy*. Austin was played by Tom Cruise (an Oscar-winning performance); Dr. Evil by Kevin Spacey (another Oscar-winning performance) and Mini-Me by Danny DeVito (a mini-Oscar-winning performance). The part of Dixie Normous – small-town FBI agent and single mother – was played by Gwyneth Paltrow.

The gala premiere of *Austinpussy* at Mann's Chinese Theatre in Los Angeles was attended by all the stars of the film, as well as celebrities such as Britney Spears.

Austinpussy wasn't the first attempt at making an Austin Powers movie. Various directors had attempted, over the years, to bring Austin Powers to the big screen, but only Steven Spielberg made a success of it. Previous Austin Powers films, such as *Middle Name: Danger*, *You Only Floss Twice*, *Four Eyes Only* and the Bollywood epic *From India With Affection*, are now only available on CD-I and as a limited edition laserdisc box set.

'No offence, Sir Stevie, but you gotta have mojo, baby! Yeah!'
AUSTIN POWERS

'Watch out,
Mr Powers –
this is one
doctor who
DOES make
house calls!'

KEVIN SPACEY AS DR. EVIL

Austin Powers: 'I can't believe
Sir Steven Spielberg, the
grooviest film-maker in the
history of cinema, is making a
movie of my life! Smashing baby, yeah!'

Scotty – Don't!

Semi- evil

Quasi-evil

THE CONTINUING saga of Scott Evil and his overwhelming disdain for his father continues as Dr. Evil gathers everyone together after his escape from prison. Dr. Evil begins describing his latest plot to replace the previously failed 'Preparation A-G' plans.

During Frau's conjugal/informational visit to Dr. Evil in 'lockdown', she informs Scott's dad that he does indeed want to take over the family business. So much so, that he has even started losing his hair. Dr. Evil is overwhelmed and delighted.

As Dr. Evil and his cohorts gather in the submarine lair, Dr. Evil is shocked into silence at the sight of his son's disappearing hair. Scott presents Dr. Evil with his long awaited evil contraption – a tank full of sharks with laserbeams attached to their heads. Choked up with emotion, Dr. Evil welcomes his newly-evil son to sit next to him as he conducts his meeting. Mini-Me is asked to 'move down the bench' and eventually to move on out of the room.

'Why not just call it Operation Ass Cream? You ass...'

SCOTT EVIL

The Diet Coke™ of evil – just one calorie – not evil enough

SCOTT'S HAIR

Once he had made the decision to follow in his father's footsteps, Scott found to his dismay that the Evil side of his genetic heritage began to make itself felt.

'Overall, Preparation H
eels good on the whole.'
DR. EVIL

'es, Preparation H does
eel good… on the hole.'
SCOTT

When Mr. Roboto – the Japanese industrialist who designed many of Dr. Evil's evil devices – demanded a bonus for his work, it was Scott, rather than Dr. Evil, who dumped him into the tank. He was learning fast, and even began to imitate his father's trademark 'little finger' gesture.

But just when he thought he had earned his father's love – just when it seemed like a good time to become evil, and see the Powers family finally get incinerated, it's revealed that your father was actually adopted by Belgians after a failed car bombing attempt on the Powers family! All along, Dr. Evil never knew the true roots of his birth family which include his long-lost brother – none other than (gasp) – AUSTIN POWERS.

When Dr. Evil realised that he and Austin needed each other, and willingly collaborated in the foiling of his own evil scheme, Scott was incredulous. He had spent years being told that he wasn't evil enough, and now his father had turned good in a moment.

Scott Evil ended up alone in his father's old Hollywood lair, dreaming of how he might rebuild his father's evil empire – and make it even more evil than before.

Whereas his father spent seven years at evil medical school, Scott's evil tendencies are entirely genetic.

Dr. Evil: 'Take it down a notch, okay Scott?'

Mojo Motors

It's a Mini, sort of. Gr8 numberpl8

Austin's personalised car started life as an E-type Jaguar, but extensive and expensive modification led to its reclassification as a one-off Shaguar. The car's number plate – SWINGER – was issued to Austin as a special 'Thank-you' to him from the British Government.

Austin had the Shaguar re-sprayed in a Union Jack paint scheme, partly as a tribute to Her Majesty the Queen.

Special features of the Shaguar include a communications panel in the dashboard, through which Austin can maintain face-to-face communications with Basil Exposition, Head of British Intelligence, and a remote control driving system which allows Austin to drive the car whilst, for instance, falling through the air fighting ninja assassins.

British Intelligence provided Austin Powers with a heavily modified Volkswagon Beetle to aid him in his mission to prevent Dr. Evil from stealing his mojo. The modifications were partly to do with the paint scheme – a rainbow-coloured whirl of stars and clouds – but more to do with the fitting of an experimental time-travel device which allowed the car to travel back to 1969.

The modifications to the Volkswagon resulted in some problems with the handling. When he first took the controls, Austin managed to destroy hundreds of thousands of British pounds of equipment by reversing into it before he could work out the gears. At least, that was his excuse.

'You know, it's remarkable how much England looks in no way like Southern California.'

AUSTIN POWERS

Remote control mechanism, somewhere in there

106

New Shaguar XK8 for the 2002 Austin

Same old low-key paintjob

PIMPMOBILE

When it became necessary for Austin Powers to travel back in time in search of his kidnapped father, British Intelligence felt that a psychedelic Volkswagen would be a little conspicuous in 1977 New York. Basil Exposition therefore authorised the installation of the entire time-travel device in a discreet Lincoln Towncar of the period.

Fully reclining seats, know what I mean?

Heated windscreen (to keep the feet of Austin's female passengers warm)

...t hand drive for ...n British roads

Picture phone thingy for Basil to stay in touch

Dr. Evil's Evil Plots

DR. EVIL'S first few ideas for obtaining vast sums of money illegally, following his return to crime in 1997, were… problematic. History had made them all redundant and he had to go back to what he knew best – grandiose schemes involving lots of henchmen, vast lairs in exotic locations and complex (and easily broken) technology.

Project Vulcan was Dr. Evil's first big project after retaking control of his evil organisation in 1997. Having stolen a nuclear warhead – his speciality – he threatened to send it plunging into the core of the planet using a subterranean torpedo system. The resulting volcanic eruptions would cover the Earth's surface in lava – unless Dr. Evil received one hundred billion dollars in ransom money.

Travelling back in time, Dr. Evil installed a gigantic laser on the moon, intending to use it to destroy whatever city he chose unless the President of the United States paid him one hundred billion dollars.

Having discovered that a Dutch metallurgist named Johann Van Der Smut had designed a cold fusion reactor, Dr. Evil devised a plan to use the reactor to power a 'tractor beam' that could drag a meteorite towards the Earth. The meteorite would hit the polar ice cap, melting it and flooding all the cities of the Earth – unless Dr. Evil was paid one hundred trillion yen.

'Oh hell, let's just do what we always do – hijack nuclear weapons and hold the world hostage.'

Dr. Evil

Dr. Evil: 'After I destroy Washington I will destroy another major city every hour on the hour – that is, unless you pay me… one hundred billion dollars!'
US President: 'Dr. Evil, that much money simply doesn't exist. I don't think one hundred billion is even a number. It's like saying "I want a kajillion bajillion dollars."'

Dr. Evil: 'Here's the plan – we get the warhead and we hold the world ransom… for one million dollars!'
Number Two: 'Don't you think maybe we should ask for more than a million dollars? A million dollars isn't exactly a lot of money these days.'

Dr. Evil: 'Congratulations numbnuts – you've succeeded in turning me into a frickin' jack-in-the-box."

From the Desk of Dr. Evil

Blackmail Royal Family with evidence of Prince Charles's infidelity **POINTLESS**

Carrot Top film project **ABANDONED**

Project Vulcan **FAILED**

Destroy ozone layer and flood planet with radiation **POINTLESS**

Steal Austin Powers' mojo **FAILED**

Alan Parsons Project **FAILED**

Preparation H **FAILED**

Human organ trafficking plot **LOOKS PROMISING**

Dr. Evil: 'As you all know, every diabolical scheme I've ever hatched has been thwarted by Austin Powers. And why is that, ladies and gentlemen?'
Scott Evil: 'Because you never kill him when you get the chance, and you're a dope?'

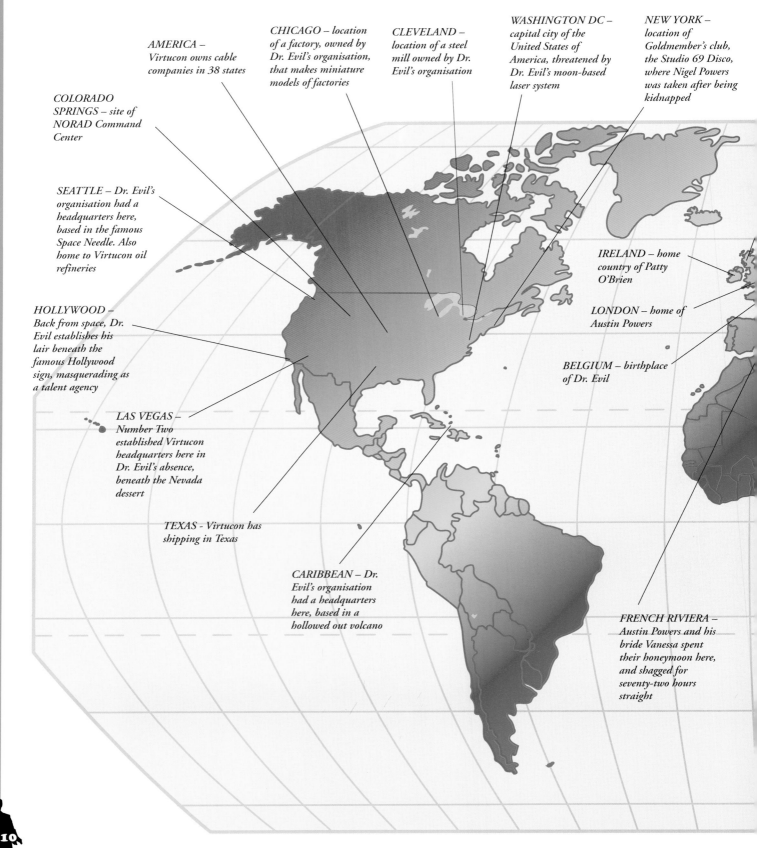

AMERICA – Virtucon owns cable companies in 38 states

CHICAGO – location of a factory, owned by Dr. Evil's organisation, that makes miniature models of factories

CLEVELAND – location of a steel mill owned by Dr. Evil's organisation

WASHINGTON DC – capital city of the United States of America, threatened by Dr. Evil's moon-based laser system

NEW YORK – location of Goldmember's club, the Studio 69 Disco, where Nigel Powers was taken after being kidnapped

COLORADO SPRINGS – site of NORAD Command Center

SEATTLE – Dr. Evil's organisation had a headquarters here, based in the famous Space Needle. Also home to Virtucon oil refineries

IRELAND – home country of Patty O'Brien

LONDON – home of Austin Powers

HOLLYWOOD – Back from space, Dr. Evil establishes his lair beneath the famous Hollywood sign, masquerading as a talent agency

BELGIUM – birthplace of Dr. Evil

LAS VEGAS – Number Two established Virtucon headquarters here in Dr. Evil's absence, beneath the Nevada dessert

TEXAS - Virtucon has shipping in Texas

CARIBBEAN – Dr. Evil's organisation had a headquarters here, based in a hollowed out volcano

FRENCH RIVIERA – Austin Powers and his bride Vanessa spent their honeymoon here, and shagged for seventy-two hours straight

HOLLAND –
home country of
Goldmember

SWEDEN – home
country of Austin's
nanny, who cared for
him until the age of
twenty-four

...SGOW – home
...a of Fat Bastard

GERMANY – home
country of Frau
Farbissina

KREPLACHISTAN –
breakaway Russian
republic who are
desperately attempting to
get rid of their nuclear
warheads but who
sometimes lose them to
the wrong people

TOKYO – location of
Roboto Industries, the
organisation that
provided Dr. Evil
with the hardware for
most of his evil
schemes

DUTCH EAST
INDIES – Austin
once caught a sexually
transmitted disease
here during shore
leave

RANGOON – where
Dr. Evil spent his
summers as a child

KOREA – home country
of Random Task

Epilogue

STILL LOOKING for more information, are you? If you're reading this, it is merely because I have decided to spare you, despite your insolence.

It's not easy being evil – or staying that way as you can see. Being raised by Belgians, you'd think it would be... So my arch-nemesis, Austin Powers defeated me a few times. So frickin' what? Despite my failed plots to achieve world domination, I've still done more than your average evil doctor... Let's see – I've been everywhere from outer space to jail, time travelled to different decades, been cloned, and watched my son lose his un-evil attitude as well as his hair. Very Norman Rockwell, if you will.

I should warn you, however, that, as you prepare to close this book, I have one last deviant plan. I have rigged the back cover of this book so that the reader cannot close it. If you close the book, you will be sprayed with liquid hot magma.

There is, of course one way out of it. I will activate the radio signal which will render this book harmless if you send me (via the publishers of this book) the following:

All of your carbon paper and typewriter ribbons. All of them. Every last bit you can find. Oh, and any slide rules you got, too.

These will form an integral part of my next plan to take over... well... you'll just have to wait and find out...

What?

Number Two has just informed me that nobody uses carbon paper any more. Or typewriters. Or slide rules. Shit.

Think this is frickin' over? How 'bout NO?!

Cast lists

AUSTIN POWERS
International Man Of Mystery

Mike Myers	Austin Danger Powers
	Dr. Evil
Elizabeth Hurley	Vanessa Kensington
Michael York	Basil Exposition
Mimi Rogers	Mrs. Kensington
Robert Wagner	Number Two
Seth Green	Scott Evil
Fabiana Udenio	Alotta Fagina
Mindy Sterling	Frau Farbissina
Paul Dillon	Patty O'Brien
Charles Napier	Commander Gilmour
Will Ferrell	Mustafa
Joann Richter	'60s Model
Anastasia Sakelaris	'60s Model
Afifi Alaouie	'60s Model
Monet Mazur	Mod Girl
Clint Howard	Radar Operator Ritter
Elya Baskin	General Borschevsky
Carlton Lee Russell	Gary Coleman
Daniel Weaver	Vanilla Ice
Neil Mullarkey	Quartermaster Clerk
Lea Sullivan I	Go-Go Dancer
Chekeshka Van Putten	Go-Go Dancer
Heather Marie Marsden	Go-Go Dancer
Sarah Smith	Go-Go Dancer
Laura Payne-Gabriel	Go-Go Dancer
Joe Son	Random Task
Tyde Kierny	Las Vegas Tourist
Larry Thomas I	Casino Dealer
Tom Arnold	Texan Businessman
Cheryl Bartel	Fembot
Cindy Margolis	Fembot
Donna W. Scott	Fembot
Barbara Ann Moore	Fembot
Cynthia Lamontagne	Fembot
Brian George	UN Secretary
Kaye Wade	Mrs. Exposition
Steve Monroe	Son
Vince Melocchi	Dad
Patrick Bristow	Virtucon Tour Guide Bolton
Jim McMullan	American UN Representative
Robin Gammell	British UN Representative
Ted Kairys	Eastern European Technician
Burt Bacharach	Himself

AUSTIN POWERS
The Spy Who Shagged Me

Mike Myers	Austin Danger Powers
	Dr. Evil
	Fat Bastard
Heather Graham	Felicity Shagwell
Michael York	Basil Exposition
Robert Wagner	Number Two
Rob Lowe	Young Number Two
Seth Green	Scott Evil
Mindy Sterling	Frau Farbissina
Verne Troyer	Mini-Me
Elizabeth Hurley	Mrs. Vanessa Powers
Gia Carides	Robin Spitz Swallows
Oliver Muirhead	British Colonel
George Cheung	Chinese Teacher
Jeffrey Meng	Chinese Student (Wang)
Muse Watson	The Klansman
Scott Cooper	Bobby
Douglas Fisher	Man (Pecker)
Kevin Cooney	NORAD Colonel
Clint Howard	Johnson Ritter
Brian Hooks	Pilot
David Koechner	Co-Pilot
Frank Clem	Guitarist with Willie Nelson
Herb Mitchell	Sergeant
Steve Eastin	Umpire
Jane Carr	Woman (Pecker)
Kevin Durand	Bazooka Marksman Joe
Melissa Justin	Chick #1 at Party
Nicholas Walker	Captain of the Guard
Stephen Hibbert	Inept Magma Chamber Guard
David Coy	Carnaby Street Band Member
David Crigger	Carnaby Street Band Member
Tom Ehlen	Carnaby Street Band Member
Dennis Wilson	Carnaby Street Band Member
Eric Winzenried	Private Army Soldier
Tim Bagley	Friendly Dad
Colton James	Friendly Son
Michael G. Hagerty	Peanut Vendor
Jack Kehler	Circus Barker
Kirk Ward	Soldier
Jeff Garland	Cyclops
Rachel Wilson	Autograph Seeker
Jennifer Coolidge	Woman at Football Game

John Mahon	NATO Colonel
Michael James McDonald	NATO Soldier
Jeanette Miller	Teacher
Mary Jo Smith	Una Brau
Carrie Ann Inaba	Felicity Dancer #1
Jennifer L. Hamilton	Felicity Dancer #2
Ayesha Orange	Felicity Dancer #3
Natalie Willes	Felicity Dancer #4
John R. Corella	Party Dancer #1
Alison Faulk	Party Dancer #2
Michelle Elkin	Party Dancer #3
Shealan Spencer	Party Dancer #4
Tovaris Wilson	Party Dancer #5
Mark Bringleson	Andy Warhol
Bree Turner	Dancer #1
Marisa Gilliam	Dancer #2
Mark Meismer	Dancer #3
Sal Vassallo	Dancer #4
Jason Yribar	Dancer #5
Chekeshka Van Putten	Go-Go Dancer #1
Tara Mouri	Go-Go Dancer #2
Gigi Yazicioglu	Go-Go Dancer #3
Sarah Smith	Scene Break Dancer
Faune A. Chambers	Scene Break Dancer
Gabriel Page	Scene Break Dancer
Jim Boensch	Queen's Guard
Ron Ulstad	Chief of Staff
Tim Waters	Bill Clinton's Look-Alike
Todd M. Schultz	Jerry Springer's Bodyguard #1
Steve Wilkos	Jerry Springer's Bodyguard #2
Burt Bacharach	Himself
Elvis Costello	Himself
Will Ferrell	Mustafa
Woody Harrelson	Himself
Kristen Johnston	Ivana Humpalot
Charles Napier	General Hawk
Willie Nelson	Himself
Tim Robbins	The President
Rebecca Romijn-Stamos	Herself
Jerry Springer	Himself
Fred Willard	Mission Commander

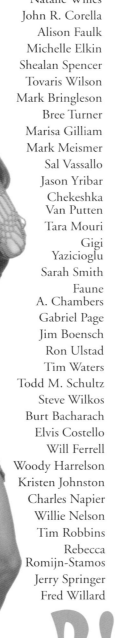

115

AUSTIN POWERS IN GOLDMEMBER

Mike Myers	Austin Danger Powers
	Dr. Evil
	Fat Bastard
	Goldmember
Beyoncé Knowles	Foxxy Cleopatra
Nichole Hiltz	French Tutor
Michael York	Basil Exposition
Michael Caine	Captain Hendricks/Nigel Powers
Seth Green	Scott Evil
Eddie Adams	Young Basil Exposition
Robert Wagner	Number Two
Mindy Sterling	Frau Farbissina
Verne Troyer	Mini-Me
Tom Cruise	Himself
Danny DeVito	Himself
Gwyneth Paltrow	Herself
Quincy Jones	Himself
Ozzy Osbourne	Himself
Kevin Spacey	Himself
Fred Savage	Number Three/The Mole
Burt Bacharach	Himself
Debbie Lee Carrington	School Girl Dancer
Kevin Cooney	General Clark
India Dupre	Belinda
Evan Farmer	Young Number Two
Aaron Himelstein	Young Austin Powers
Susanna Hoffs	Gillian Shagwell (Ming Tea)
Clint Howard	Johnson Ritter
Carrie Ann Inaba	Fook Yu
Stuart D. Johnson	Manny Stixman (Ming Tea)
Nina Kaczorowski	Goldmember's Henchwoman
Linda Kim	Geisha Secretary
Nathan Lane	Mysterious Disco Man
Rob Lowe	Young Number Two
Diane Mizota	Fook Mi
Jack Osbourne	Himself
Kelly Osbourne	Herself
Sharon Osbourne	Herself
Kinga Phillips	Austin's mom
Jim Piddock	Headmaster
Riley Schmidt	Partygoer
Britney Spears	Herself
Steven Spielberg	Himself
Matthew Sweet	Sid Belvedere (Ming Tea)
John Travolta	Himself
Christopher Ward	Trevor Aigberth (Ming Tea)
Josh Zuckerman	Young Dr. Evil

Smashing! AND I'M SPENT.